荆 州 楚 玉
湖北荆州出土战国时期楚国玉器

JINGZHOU CHU JADES
The Jades of the Chu State of the Warring States
Period Unearthed in Jingzhou Prefecture, Hubei

JINGZHOU CHU JADES

THE JADES OF THE CHU STATE OF THE WARRING STATES PERIOD UNEARTHED IN JINGZHOU PREFECTURE, HUBEI

EDITED BY JINGZHOU MUSEUM

荆州楚玉

湖北荆州出土战国时期楚国玉器

荆州博物馆　编著

文物出版社

编 委 会
EDITORIAL COMMITTEE

目 录
CONTENTS

33. 卷云纹玉环
Jade Ring with Cloud Pattern

34. 卷云纹玉环
Jade Ring with Cloud Pattern

35. 卷云纹玉环
Jade Ring with Cloud Pattern

36. 勾连云纹玉环
Jade Ring with Cloud Pattern

37. "S" 形云纹玉环
Jade Ring with S-shaped Cloud Pattern

38. 龙纹玉环
Jade Ring with Dragon Pattern

39. 蟠虺纹琉璃环
Glass Ring with Coiled Dragon Pattern

40. 鸡血玛瑙环
Chalcedony Rings (2 pieces)

41. 玛瑙环
Chalcedony Ring

42. 玛瑙环
Chalcedony Ring

43. 水晶环
Rock Crystal Ring

44. 谷纹玉璜
Jade *Huang*-semicircular Pendant with Grain Pattern

45. 谷纹玉璜
A Pair of Jade *Huang*-semicircular Pendants with Grain Pattern

46. 谷纹玉璜
A Pair of Jade *Huang*-semicircular Pendants with Grain Pattern

47. 谷纹玉璜
Jade *Huang*-semicircular Pendant with Grain Pattern

48. 蟠虺纹玉璜
Jade *Huang*-semicircular Pendant with Coiled Dragon Pattern

49. 蟠虺纹玉璜
Jade *Huang*-semicircular Pendant with Coiled Dragon Pattern

50. 蟠虺纹玉璜
Jade *Huang*-semicircular Pendant with Coiled Dragon Pattern

51. 透雕龙凤虺纹玉璜
Jade *Huang*-semicircular Pendant with Dragon and Phoenix Pattern in Openwork

52. 勾连云纹玉璜
Jade *Huang*-semicircular Pendant with Cloud Pattern

53. 勾连云纹玉璜
A Pair of Jade *Huang*-semicircular Pendants with Cloud Pattern

54. 勾连云纹玉璜
A Pair of Jade *Huang*-semicircular Pendants with Cloud Pattern

55. "S" 形云纹玉璜
Jade *Huang*-semicircular Pendant with S-shaped Cloud Pattern

56. 几何形云纹玉璜
Jade *Huang*-semicircular Pendant with Cloud Pattern

57. 双龙首谷纹玉璜
Jade *Huang*-semicircular Pendant with Double-head-dragon and Grain Pattern

58. 双龙首谷纹玉璜
Jade *Huang*-semicircular Pendant with Double-head-dragon Pattern

59. 双龙首勾连云纹玉璜
Jade *Huang*-semicircular Pendant with Double-head-dragon Pattern

60. 双龙首玉璜
Jade *Huang*-semicircular Pendant with Dragon Heads

61. 玉璜
Jade *Huang*-semicircular Pendant

62. 玉璜
Jade *Huang*-semicircular Pendant

63. 玉璜
Jade *Huang*-semicircular Pendant

64. 玉璜
Jade *Huang*-semicircular Pendant

65. 玉璜
Jade *Huang*-semicircular Pendant

66. 玉璜
Jade *Huang*-semicircular Pendant

67. 玉璜
Jade *Huang*-semicircular Pendant

68. 玉璜
A Pair of Jade *Huang*-semicircular Pendants

69. 玉璜
Jade *Huang*-semicircular Pendant

70. 龙首形玛瑙璜
Chalcedony *Huang*-semicircular Pendant with Dragon Heads Pattern

71. 龙首形玛瑙璜
Chalcedony *Huang*-semicircular Pendant with Dragon Heads Pattern

72. 龙形玉珮
A Pair of Jade Dragon-shaped Pendants

73. 龙形玉珮
Jade Dragon-shaped Pendants (2 pieces)

74. 龙形玉珮
Jade Dragon-shaped Pendant

75. 龙形玉珮
A Pair of Jade Dragon-shaped Pendants

76. 龙形玉珮
A Pair of Jade Dragon-shaped Pendants

77. 龙形玉珮
A Pair of Jade Dragon-shaped Pendants

78. 龙形玉珮
Jade Dragon-shaped Pendant

79. 龙形玉珮
Jade Dragon-shaped Pendant

80. 龙形玉珮
Jade Dragon-shaped Pendant

81. 龙形玉珮
A Pair of Jade Dragon-shaped Pendants

82. 龙形玉珮
A Pair of Jade Dragon-shaped Pendants

83. 龙形玉珮
Jade Dragon-shaped Pendant

84. 龙形玉珮
Jade Dragon-shaped Pendant

85. 龙形玉珮
A Pair of Jade Dragon-shaped Pendants

86. 龙形玉珮
Jade Dragon-shaped Pendant

87. 龙形玉珮
A Pair of Jade Dragon-shaped Pendants

88. 龙形玉珮
A Pair of Jade Dragon-shaped Pendants

89. 龙形玉珮
Jade Dragon-shaped Pendant

90. 龙形玉珮
Jade Dragon-shaped Pendant

91. 龙形玉珮
Jade Dragon-shaped Pendant

92. 龙形玉珮
Jade Dragon-shaped Pendant

93. 龙形玉珮
A Pair of Jade Dragon-shaped Pendants

94. 龙形玉珮
Jade Dragon-shaped Pendant

95. 龙形玉珮
A Pair of Jade Dragon-shaped Pendants

96. 龙形玉珮
Jade Dragon-shaped Pendant

97. 龙形玉珮
A Pair of Jade Dragon-shaped Pendants

98. 龙形玉珮
Jade Dragon-shaped Pendant

99. 龙形玉珮
Jade Dragon-shaped Pendant

100. 龙形玉珮
Jade Dragon-shaped Pendant

101. 龙形玉珮
Jade Dragon-shaped Pendant

102. 龙形玉珮
Jade Dragon-shaped Pendant

103. 双龙形玉珮
Jade Pendant in the Shape of Double Dragons

104. 双龙形玉珮
Jade Pendant in the Shape of Double Dragons

105. 双龙形玉珮
Jade Pendant in the Shape of Double Dragons

106. 双龙形玉珮
Jade Pendant in the Shape of Double Dragons

107. 双龙形玉珮
Jade Pendant in the Shape of Double Dragons

108. 龙凤形玉珮
Jade Pendant in the Shape of a Dragon and a Phoenix

109. 龙凤形玉珮
Jade Pendant in the Shape of a Dragon and a Phoenix

110. 龙凤形玉珮
Jade Pendant in the Shape of a Dragon and a Phoenix

111. 双首龙形玉珮
Jade Pendant in the Shape of a Double-head-dragon

112. 龙鸟蛇形玉珮
Jade Pendant in the Shape of Dragons, Birds, and Snake

113. 神人乘龙形玉珮
Jade Pendant in the Shape of a Human Deity Riding a Dragon

114. 神人操龙形玉珮
Jade Pendant in the Shape of a Human Deity and a Dragon

115. 透雕云纹玉珮
Jade Pendant with Cloud Pattern in Openwork

116. 三角形玉饰
Jade Pendant in the Shape of a Triangle

117. 玉觿
A Pair of Jade *Xi*-bodkin Pendants

118. 玉琮
Jade *Cong*-Prismatic Cylinder

119. 玉琮
Jade *Cong*-Prismatic Cylinder

120. 蟠虺纹玉玦
Jade Slit *Jue*-earring with Coiled Dragon Pattern

121. 龙首玉带钩
Jade Belt Hook with Dragon Head Pattern

122. 龙首玉带钩
Jade Belt Hook with Dragon Head Pattern

123. 龙首玉带钩
Jade Belt Hook with Dragon Head Pattern

124. 龙首玉带钩
Jade Belt Hook with Dragon Head Pattern

荆州地区楚墓出土玉器概论

王明钦

一 荆州楚文化与荆州楚墓

荆州地处江汉平原腹地，土地宽广，河湖纵横，气候温暖，物产丰富，是人类生存与繁衍的理想场所。荆州又是长江中游的交通枢纽和南北交汇的中心，水陆交通十分便利。因此，荆州是一个历史悠久、文化绵长的地区。早在旧石器时代，荆州就有了人类活动，1992年发掘的鸡公山旧石器时代遗址，是我国第一次大面积发掘的原始人类在平原地区居住、生活的遗迹，揭示了原始人类从山区走向平原、从山洞穴居到平地起屋的发展历程。新石器时代，荆州的先民们创造了大溪—屈家岭—石家河文化，也就是古史传说中的"三苗文化"[1]，为楚文化的兴盛与繁荣奠定了坚实的基础。严文明先生指出："无论如何，著名的楚文化应是从这里孕育起来的。"[2]

我们所说的楚文化一般是指东周时期的典型楚文化，是楚民族形成、楚国建立后所创造的文化。楚族源于帝颛顼高阳，为"祝融八姓"之一，西周时期，周成王封熊绎为"楚子"，标志着楚国的正式建立。西周晚期，楚国国势逐渐强大起来，楚子熊渠第一次大胆地说："我蛮夷也，不与中国之号谥！"封三子为王，其长子熊康为句亶王，其封地就在荆州境内的江陵。春秋时期，楚国异军突起，楚武王先使"蛮夷皆率服"，后征"汉阳诸姬"，楚文王完全征服"汉阳诸姬"并击败蔡国，到楚成王时已从"土不过同"发展到"楚地千里"，楚庄王更是"观兵周郊"、"问鼎中原"，成为"春秋五霸"之一。战国时期，经过吴起变法，楚国"南平百越，北并陈蔡，西伐秦，诸侯患楚之强。"楚威王时，南灭越，北败齐，其势力遍及南部大半个中国，成为"地方五千里，带甲百万，车千乘，骑万匹"的"战国七雄"之一。

特色鲜明、辉煌灿烂的楚文化在荆州留下了丰富的文物资源。荆州是楚国强盛时期的都城所在地，以面积达16平方公里的楚故都纪南城遗址为中心，分布着4000余处古文化遗址和古墓群，其中绝大部分为楚文化遗存。纪南城、蔡桥、青山等楚国都城或宫殿基址，八岭山、纪山、马山、川店、天星观等楚国贵族墓葬群，以及熊家冢、冯家冢、平头冢、周家冢等特大型楚国王公贵族墓地，都以规模宏大、布局完整、内涵丰富、保存完好而闻名遐迩。在紧邻楚都纪南城遗址

① 俞伟超：《先楚与三苗文化的考古学推测》，《文物》1980年第10期。

② 严文明：《中国史前文化的统一性与多样性》，《文物》1987年第3期。

图一　荆州在湖北省的位置示意图

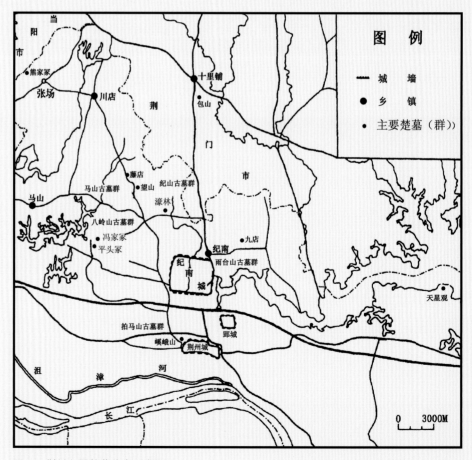

图二　荆州主要楚墓分布示意图

图三　天星观2号楚墓发掘现场

的雨台山、九店、拍马山、嵊峨山、张家山、葛陂寺、官坪、纪城等古墓群中，还分布着数以万计的中小型楚墓（图一、二）。

20世纪70年代以来，荆州一直是全国楚文化考古发掘与研究的中心。1975年全国考古界纪南城大会战，拉开了楚故都纪南城遗址与荆州楚墓发掘的序幕。几十年来，十几万平方米的楚文化遗址和5000余座楚墓的发掘，不仅为楚文化研究积累了丰富的考古资料，还出土了数以万计的珍贵文物。这些文物数量众多、种类齐全、造型别致、制作精美、装饰华丽，代表了楚文化的最高成就。尤其是楚国织绣品、漆木器、简牍、玉器、铜器等举世罕见，具有相当高的研究价值和艺术价值（图三至一一）。

荆州境内发现与发掘的楚墓，大致分为五类：第一类是特大型楚墓。其特征是规模巨大、布局完整。墓葬封土直径在100米以上，开口长宽60米以上，深度超过18米，椁室长度在15米以上，椁内分为7~9室，有多重棺椁；墓地有主墓、陪葬墓（应为夫妻异穴合葬）、大型车马坑、众多殉葬墓和祭祀坑等遗存，如熊家冢、冯家冢、平头冢等，这类墓葬的墓主身份应是楚王或最高等级的王室成员。第二类是大型楚墓。墓葬有较大的封土堆，开口长

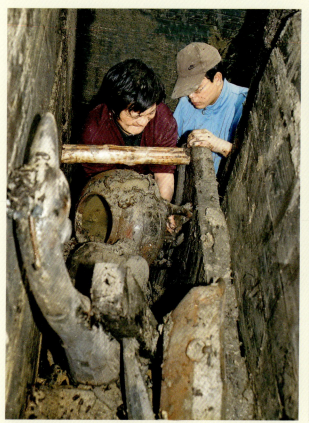

图四　天星观2号楚墓东室清理现场

图五　凤鸟花卉纹绣浅黄绢面绵袍，马山1号楚墓出土

图六　凤鸟莲花盘豆，天星观2号楚墓出土

图七　虎座凤鸟悬鼓，天星观2号楚墓出土

宽在30米以上，椁室长度在8米以上，椁内分为5~7室，有多重棺椁。布局多为家族墓地，主墓之旁分布一些陪葬墓（当为家族成员），部分有车马坑、殉葬墓，如天星观1号墓等，这类墓葬的墓主应为封君或上大夫。第三类是中型楚墓。墓葬大部分有封土，开口在10米以上，椁室长度在3~6米，椁内分3~5室，如天星观2号墓、望山1号和2号墓、滕店1号墓、秦家山2号墓、院墙湾1号墓等，这类墓葬的墓主应为下大夫或元士。第四类为小型楚墓。一般无封土，多为一棺一椁，一般是椁分2~3室，即留出头箱，有的有很窄的边箱，这类墓葬的墓主应为士。第五类为单棺墓，随葬品很少，墓主应为贫穷的士或庶人。

二 荆州楚墓出土玉器概述

不同类别的楚墓或者说不同等级的楚墓，除了规模大小外，随葬礼器、兵器、乐器以及日常用品的情况大不相同，玉器也一样。一般来说，等级越高，随葬玉器的数量越多，质量越好。荆州楚墓中第一、二、三类楚墓大多有不同数量的玉器随葬，第四类楚墓部分出土玉器，第五类楚墓则基本没有玉器随葬。这种情况表明，荆州楚墓出土玉器的情况与《礼记》所说"古之君子必佩玉"、"君子无故玉不去身"是基本相符的。当然，除了身份等级以外，随葬玉器的情况也多少会受到墓葬年代、墓主人族属等因素的影响。荆州出土玉器的楚墓有熊家冢墓地，冯家冢墓地，天星观1、2号墓，枣林岗与堆金台墓地，雨台山墓地，九店墓地，望山1、2、3、4号墓，拍马山墓地，沙冢1号墓，滕店1号墓，鸡公山墓地，杨场墓地，范家坡墓地，紫荆砖瓦厂墓地，嵝峨山墓地，张家山墓地，秦家山2号墓和院墙湾1号墓等等。兹就不同类别楚墓出土玉器的情况略举数例如下（图一二）。

第一类墓葬

熊家冢墓地 位于荆州市荆州区川店镇张场村、宗北村与当阳市河溶镇星火村交界处，东南距楚都纪南城遗址约26公里，墓地现存面积约15万平方米，由主墓、陪葬墓、殉葬墓、车马坑、祭祀坑和附属建筑组成。主墓是一座近方形、带斜坡墓道的"甲"字形竖穴土坑木椁墓，方向96°。墓道位于东侧，长36、宽6~35米。墓口东西长67、南北宽70米，墓口至椁顶板深约14.5米，椁室面积约400平方米。主墓北边为陪葬墓，规模约为主墓的四分之一；主墓的南边分布着4列24排共92座殉葬墓，排列整齐，间距、大小、方向基本一致，在陪葬墓以北发现4列10排殉葬墓，分布情况与主墓南边基本相同，但规模略小；主墓与陪葬墓的西边为车马坑，由一座长132、宽12米

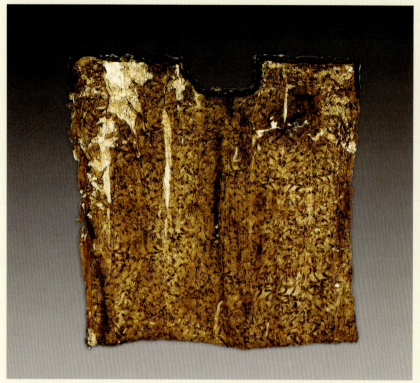

图八　蟠龙飞凤纹绣浅黄绢面衾，马山1号楚墓出土

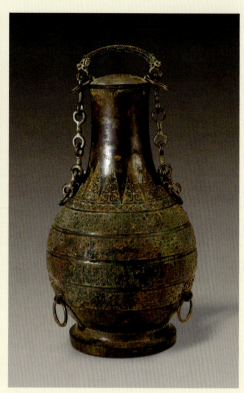

图九　铜提梁壶，马山1号楚墓出土

图一〇　铜升鼎，天星观2号楚墓出土

图一一　竹简，天星观1号楚墓出土

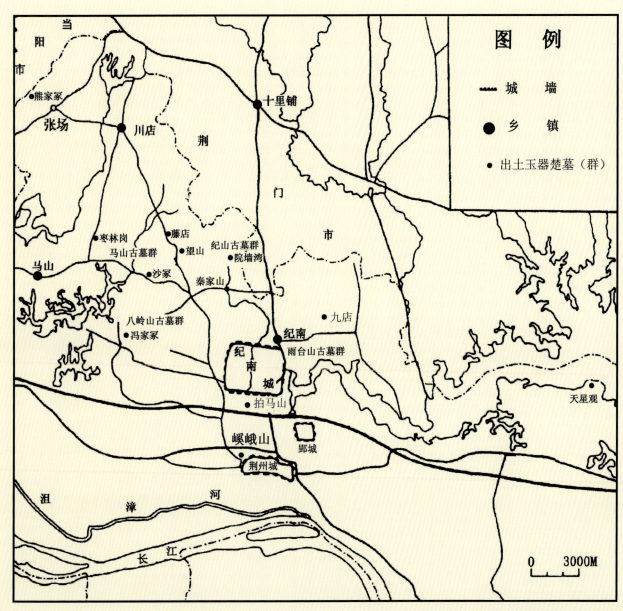

图一二 荆州出土玉器楚墓分布示意图

的大型车马坑和39座小型车马坑组成；在主墓南北两边和车马坑附近还有200
余处祭祀坑。从2006年开始，荆州博物馆发掘了50余座殉葬墓、10余处祭祀
坑、11座小型车马坑和大型车马坑的一部分，出土了近2000件玉器，另有极
少数铜器和陶器。殉葬墓中的玉器多以组玉珮的形式出现，放置于棺内，种
类有璧、环、珮、璜、珩、璧、串珠、管等，祭祀坑中主要是璧、璜，部分
车马坑中在马头部出土百余件瓜籽形玉饰片[3]（图一三至二〇）。

第二类墓葬
　　天星观1号楚墓　位于荆州市沙市区观音垱镇天星观村北部长湖南岸，西

③ 荆州博物馆：《湖北荆州熊
家冢墓地2006—2007年发掘简
报》，《文物》2009年第4期；
《湖北荆州熊家冢墓地2008年发
掘简报》，《文物》2011年第2期。

④ 湖北省荆州博物馆：《江陵天星观1号楚墓》，《考古学报》1982年第1期。

⑤ 湖北省文物考古研究所：《江陵望山与沙冢楚墓》，文物出版社，1996年。

⑥ 荆州博物馆：《湖北荆州院墙湾一号楚墓》，《文物》2008年第4期。

⑦ 荆州博物馆：《湖北荆州秦家山二号墓清理简报》，《文物》1999年第4期。

距楚故都纪南城约24公里。这里东西向排列着5座有封土的大型墓葬，天星观1号墓是其中最大的一座。1978年，荆州博物馆对其进行了发掘。该墓封土大部分已遭破坏，墓口南北长41.2、东西宽37.2、深12.2米，墓道在南，长18.8米，葬具为两椁两棺，椁长8.2、宽7.5米，椁内分为7室，其中6室被严重盗扰，仅北室保存完好，出土青铜礼器、兵器、乐器、车马器、漆木竹器、简牍、玉器等随葬品2400多件。残存玉器22件，其中玉璧16件，玉俑6件，皆放置于棺室内④（图二一至二三）。

第三类墓葬

望山2号楚墓 位于荆州市荆州区马山镇望山村，东南距楚都纪南城遗址约7公里。1965年，为配合漳河水库修渠工程，湖北省文物管理委员会、文物工作队进行了抢救性发掘。该墓墓口长11.84、宽9.43、深6.69米。墓道在东，长8.6、宽1.7~3.7米。葬具为一椁三棺，椁长5.08、宽2.96米，椁内分为3室。该墓虽早期被盗，仍出土陶器、铜器、漆木器、玉石器、竹简等文物617件，其中玉石器69件，有玉璧、玉璜、玉珮、玉带钩、玛瑙环、水晶珠等，其中璧、环、珮出于内棺，其余出于头箱⑤（图二四）。

院墙湾1号楚墓 位于荆州市荆州区马山镇濠林村，南距楚故都纪南城约4.5公里。2006年3月，由于被盗掘破坏，荆州博物馆进行了抢救性发掘。该墓墓口残长7.9、残宽6.35米，墓道在东边，残长5.12米。葬具为一椁重棺，椁长4.4、宽2.2米，椁内分为3室。出土残存随葬品129件，有陶器、铜器、漆木器、玉器、锡器等。其中玉器29件，有环、璧、璜、牙形饰、扁管、珮、印等，皆放置于棺内⑥（图二五至二八）。

秦家山2号楚墓 位于荆州市荆州区马山镇濠林村，南距楚故都纪南城约6.5公里。1997年8月，由于遭到盗墓破坏，荆州博物馆进行了抢救性发掘。该墓为正方形，边长14.8米，深8.2米，墓道在东，长14.5、宽4.5~5米；葬具为一椁三棺，椁长4.9、宽3.45米，椁内分为3室。由于被盗扰严重，残存陶器、漆器、骨器、铜器、玉器等44件，其中玉器6件，有覆面、璜、珮、笄等，皆放置于内棺墓主人头部⑦（图二九、三〇）。

第四类墓葬

雨台山166号楚墓 位于楚都纪南城遗址东面

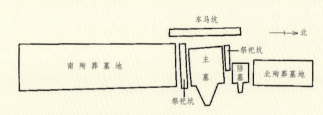

图一三 熊家冢墓地平面布局示意图

图一四 熊家冢墓地航拍图

图一五　熊家冢墓地殉葬墓区全景

图一六　熊家冢墓地车马坑区全景

图一七　熊家冢4号殉葬墓发掘现场

图二〇　熊家冢墓地33号车马坑马头部玉饰

图一八　熊家冢4号殉葬墓玉组珮出土情况

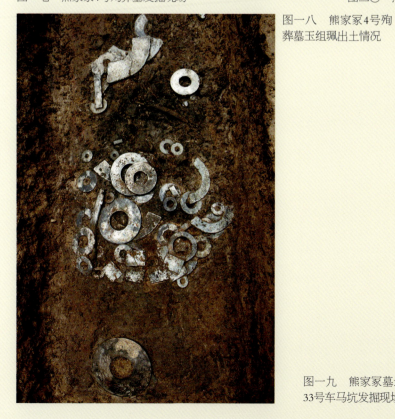

图一九　熊家冢墓地33号车马坑发掘现场

图二一　天星观1号楚墓发掘现场　　　　　　　　　　　图二二　天星观1号楚墓椁室

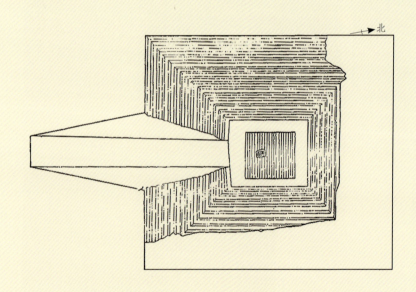

北→

图二三　天星观1号楚墓平面图

不到1公里处，1976年为配合龙桥河改道工程，由纪南城文物保护与考古发掘领导小组和荆州博物馆组成的考古队发掘。该墓为长方形，墓口长5、宽3.5米，葬具为一椁一棺。椁室长3.2、宽1.42米。出土陶器、漆木器、骨器、丝织品、玉器等20件，其中玉珮1件，放置于头箱内[8]（图三一）。

三　荆州楚墓出土玉器的年代与主要特征

　　荆州出土玉器楚墓的年代，主要集中在战国时期，尤其是战国早中期，这与荆州作为楚文化中心地位的背景是一致的。在荆州发现的春秋时期墓葬很少，我们在纪南城遗址内西北部的陕家湾，纪南城遗址东边的雨台山、九店，北边的纪城等地发掘了部分春秋时期楚墓，但墓葬数量少、规模小，一般为单棺或无椁无棺墓，出土的随葬品也很少，多为三五件小型陶器，基本没有铜器、玉器等随葬品。这种现象表明，春秋时期楚国尚未定都纪南城，虽然荆州属楚国范围，但并未成为楚国统治的核心和楚文化的中心。而到了战国时期，这种局面有了很大的改变，纪南城及其周边的建筑遗存，绝大多

⑧　湖北省荆州博物馆：《江陵雨台山楚墓》，文物出版社，1984年。

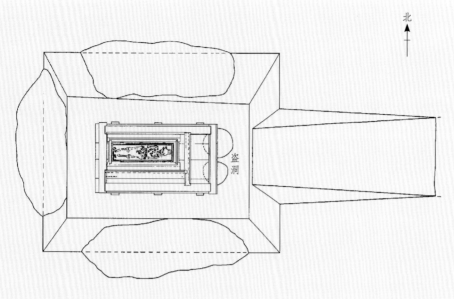

北

图二五　院墙湾1号楚墓平面图

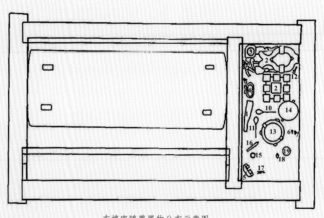

东椁室随葬器物分布示意图

1.木鸟颈　2.木镇墓兽　3.陶壶　4、5.漆耳杯　6、7.漆瑟柄　8.铜鼎足
10、11.铜匕　12.铜盖弓帽　13.陶鼎　14.陶敦　15.玉环　16.铜刻刀
17.锡棍（2件）　18.木鸟首　19.铜镜

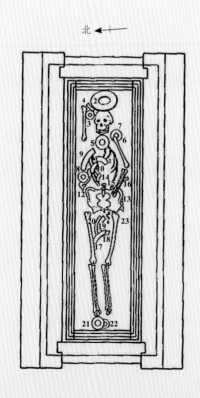

北　←

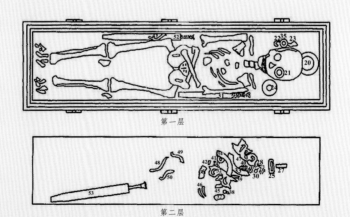

第一层

第二层

内棺随葬器物分布示意图

20.玉环　21、24、44.玉璧　22.双首龙形玉珮　23、31、32.回首龙形玉珮　25.多首龙形玉珮
27、41.玉璜　28.包金料管　30.琉璃珠　33、34、45.玉璜　36.神人操两龙形玉珮
37.龙、鸟、鱼形玉珮　38.鎏金铜带钩　39.昂首龙形玉珮　40.吐舌龙形玉珮　42.玉印
46.玉牙形饰（2件）　47～50.无足龙形玉珮　52、53.铜剑

1、2、3、5、7、8、21、22.玉璧　4、6、9～10、14～20.玉璜
12、13.玉珮　23.陶管状饰

图二四　望山2号楚墓内棺器物分布图　　　图二六　院墙湾1号楚墓椁室及棺内器物分布图

图二七　院墙湾1号楚墓发掘现场　　　　　　　图二八　院墙湾1号楚墓玉器出土情况

数是战国时期，与此相应，荆州发掘的楚墓，也以战国时期的为主。值得一提的是，战国早期的楚墓数量虽不少，但规模大、级别高的也不多。这与当时楚国的国力和地位也是一致的。春秋时期，楚国经过一系列的兼并战争，虽然楚庄王"观兵周郊"、"问鼎中原"，并在邲之战中一举击败称霸中原几十年的晋国，成为"春秋五霸"之一，但到了战国早期，由于各国纷纷变法，楚国疆域虽大，但实力并不是最强的，而且还发生了"盗杀楚声王"的事件。直到楚悼王时任命吴起为令尹，实行"吴起变法"，才使楚国真正强大起来，迎来了"宣威盛世"，成为"战国七雄"之一。这一时期正是战国中期。因此，荆州境内的大中型楚墓，绝大多数是这一时期，荆州玉器出土最多的楚墓，也在这一时期。到了战国晚期，尤其是公元前278年秦将白起攻陷楚都纪南城之后，楚顷襄王北徙陈郢（河南淮阳），公元前241年，楚考烈王又东迁寿郢（安徽寿春）。公元前223年，秦灭楚这一时期，楚都纪南城是城废人空，再没有楚国高级贵族了，虽然这一时期在荆州既有秦人的墓葬，也有楚遗民的墓葬，但规模都不大，等级也不高，很少有玉器随葬。

值得注意的是，在秦和西汉早期的墓葬中，也有战国楚玉随葬，如纪南城内东南隅的凤凰山墓地、纪南城外东南边的谢家桥墓地等，这与玉器兼具珍宝与艺术性的特性、常被收藏与传承是相关的。实际上，在荆州战国楚墓中也经常有春秋时期玉器出土，如熊家冢墓地等，这与秦汉时期墓葬出土战国楚玉的情况是相似的。

还有一个值得注意的现象，荆州楚墓出土玉器中，除典型的楚式玉器外，还有相当多的中原式玉器，部分越式玉器、少量秦式玉器和个别东夷式玉器。

楚族源于中原，楚立国初期的文化与中原文化是一体的，春秋战国时期，楚国虽然异军突起，形成了自己独特的文化风格，但中原文化因素一直存在，楚玉也往往兼具中原与楚式的双重特征，因此，典型的中原式玉器在楚地一直存在，在望山2号、秦家山2号等楚墓中都有中原式玉器出土。

战国时期，楚都纪南城附近有不少越人定居生活，我们发掘了一些典型的越人墓葬，出土了不少越式铜鼎、铜矛和日用陶器，也有不少越式玉器，在雨台山516、535，九店143、295、617、715号墓以及嵊峨山墓地的部分墓葬中都发现了以圈点纹为主要特征的越式玉璧和石璧。

荆州楚墓中出土的秦式玉器数量很少，目前仅在秦家山2号楚墓和熊家冢5、54号殉葬墓中发现了以阴刻硬直的几何形单线纹为主要特征的秦式玉璜和玉珩。

东夷式玉器更少，目前仅在熊家冢墓地殉葬墓中发现两件，质地皆为淡黄色玛瑙，器形为拱桥形璜，与山东临淄郎家庄一号东周殉葬墓中出土的角质珩类似。

荆州楚墓出土的玉器，按用途主要分为礼玉、佩玉和葬玉三大类。礼玉主要用于各种礼仪场合，如祭祀、朝聘、宴飨和婚丧等，如熊家冢墓地祭祀坑中出土的玉璧、玉璜，天星观1号墓出土的玉戈等。佩玉是墓主人生前佩戴的玉器，数量和品种都很多，也是荆州大中型楚墓中最为常见的，有珮、璧、环、璜、珩、坠、冲牙、扁管、珠、带钩、剑饰等。葬玉是专为下葬时保护与装敛尸体制作的，如秦家山2号墓出土的玉覆面。当然，生前使用的佩玉也可用作葬玉，如果考察秦家山2号楚墓出土玉器情况，那么除玉覆面以外，两件玉珮和两件玉璜并非作为佩玉使用，而是系于覆盖墓主人面部的丝质冥目四角，以起固定作用，实际上也是当作葬玉在使用。

图二九　秦家山2号楚墓发掘现场　　　图三〇　秦家山2号楚墓棺内玉履面出土情况

北

1.虎座飞鸟　2、4.陶壶　3.竹筒　5、6.陶鼎　7.漆厄　8、9.陶簠　10.陶镣壶　12.陶环耳鼎　13、19.陶豆　14.陶罍　15.玉佩饰　18.鹿角（2件）

图三一　雨台山166号楚墓器物分布图

A BRIEF INTRODUCTION OF THE JADES UNEARTHED FROM THE TOMBS OF THE CHU STATE IN JINGZHOU PREFECTURE

(Summary)

Wang Mingqin

Jingzhou is the location of the capital of the Chu State in the Eastern Zhou Period when it was at its climax. Centered by the Jinan City Site covering an area of 16 sq km, more than 4000 ancient cultural remains and ancient burials are scattered, most of which are that of the Chu Culture. In the recent several decades, the excavations of the cultural remains covering more than a dozen hectares and five thousand tombs accumulated plenty of data for the Chu Culture researches and recovered tens of thousands of valuable cultural relics. These cultural relics have comprehensive varieties, original shapes and elaborate making techniques as well as brilliant decorative patterns, representing the highest level of Chu Culture. The textiles and embroideries, lacquer and wooden wares, bamboo slips and wooden tablets, jades and bronzes among them are rarely seen in the world and have uncountable academic, artistic and appreciating values.

The tombs of the Chu State in Jingzhou Prefecture yielding jades are concentrated in the Warring-States Period especially its early and middle phases, which coincided with its position as the center of the Chu Culture at that time. The tombs of the Spring and Autumn Period found in Jingzhou Prefecture are not only few in number and small in scale, but also yielded insufficient grave goods, most of which are only potteries, bronzes and jades are almost absent in these tombs. This situation shows that in the Spring and Autumn Period, the Chu State did not set its capital in Jingzhou area and although this area had been the territory of the Chu State, it was still not its political and cultural center. Down to the Warring States Period, this situation sharply changed. The architectural remains in and nearby the Jinan City Site are mostly that of the Warring States Period, so are the tombs of the Chu State excavated in Jingzhou Prefecture. However, in the early Warring States Period, the tombs were numerous but the ones with large sizes and high ranks were also very few, which matched the state power and position of the Chu State at that time. In the Spring and Autumn Period, through a series of annexing wars, the Chu State became one of the "Five Hegemonies". In the reign of King Dao, Wu Qi was assigned as the prime minister and enforced the "Wu Qi's Political Reform", which made the Chu State really strong and enter the "flourishing age of the Xuan and Wei (the reigns of Kings Xuan and Wei)", finally became one of the "Seven Powers" of the Warring States Period. All of these occurred in the mid Warring States Period, and most of the large- and medium-sized tombs found to date in Jingzhou Prefecture belonged to this phase, and most of the jades of the Chu State are also unearthed from the tombs of this phase. In late Warring States Period, especially after General Bai Qi occupied Jinan City, the capital of the Chu State, in 278 BC, King Qingxiang of the Chu State moved his capital northward to the Chen Ying (present-day Huaiyang, Henan) and King Kaolie moved his capital again eastward to Shou Ying (present-day Shouzhou, Anhui) in 241 BC, down to 223 BC when the Chu State was annexed by the Qin State (thereafter Qin Dynasty), the Jinan City was abandoned and ruined and there were not aristocrats of the Chu State living here. The tombs of the Qin people and the adherents of the annexed Chu State in this period were found in Jingzhou Prefecture, but they were small and low in ranks and seldom yielding jades.

It is noticeable that in the tombs of the Qin and early Western Han Dynasties, jades of the Chu State in the Warring States Period could also be found, such as in the tombs of the Fenghuangshan Cemetery in the southeast corner of Jinan City and the Xiejiaqiao Cemetery to the southeast of Jinan City, and so on. This would be because the jades have the nature of both treasures and artworks and are usually collected and handed down. In fact, jades of the Spring and Autumn Period are also often seen in the Chu tombs of the Warring-States Period in Jingzhou, such as those in Xiongjiazhong Cemetery, and so on, which has the similar reason with the tombs of the Qin and Han Dynasties yielding jades of the Warring-States Period.

Another noticeable phenomenon is that among the jades unearthed from the tombs of the Chu State in Jingzhou, there are many jades of the Central Plains style as well as that of the Yue and Qin styles and some of the Dongyi (Eastern Barbarians) style.

The jades unearthed from the tombs of the Chu State in Jingzhou can be classified by function into three categories, which are ritual jades, ornamental jades and burial jades. Ritual jades, such as the jade *bi*-discs and *huang*-semicircular pendants unearthed from the sacrificial pits in Xiongjiazhong Cemetery and the jade *gui*-scepter unearthed from tomb No. 1 of Tianxingguan Cemetery, were mainly used on rites and ceremonies, including sacrifices, audiences and envoy receiving ceremonies, banquets, weddings and funerals, etc. Ornamental jades are jewelries worn by the tomb occupants when they were alive, and this category have the most diversified types and the most amounts in the jades unearthed from the tombs of the Chu State in Jingzhou; the main types of the ornamental jades are plaques, *bi*-discs, rings, *huang*-semicircular pendants, horizontal pendants, eardrops, bodkin-shaped pendants, flat tubular pendants, beads, belt hooks, sword fittings, etc. Burial jades are made especially for protecting the corpse or interment, such as the jade burial mask unearthed from tomb No. 2 in Qinjiashan Cemetery. Of course, the ornamental jades used when the tomb occupant was alive could also be used as burial jades. When we observe the usage of the jades in tomb No. 2 in Qinjiashan Cemetery, we can find that in addition to the jade burial mask, the two jade plaques and two *huang*-semicircular were not used as ornaments but tied to the four corners of the silk "*mimu* (face covering)" for fasting, so they were also used as burial jades.

(Translated by Ding Xiaolei)

玉璧
Jade *Bi*

——

玉环
Jade *Huan*

——

玉璜
Jade *Huang*

——

玉珮
Jade Pendant

——

其他器形
Others

图 版
PLATES

1 谷纹玉璧
Jade *Bi*-disc with Grain Pattern

战国早期礼仪用玉
湖北省荆州市熊家冢墓地出土
直径21.3、孔径9.6、厚0.9厘米

Early Warring States Period
Excavated from Xiongjiazhong Cemetery of
Chu State in Jingzhou, Hubei Province
D. (outer) 21.3 cm, D. (inner) 9.6 cm, Th. 0.9 cm

玉质青绿色，微透明，夹点状黑色斑，边缘有少
量黄褐色沁。扁平体，正圆形，内外缘有阴刻的
轮廓线，两面碾琢谷纹。中间有几处断裂痕。

点 评
Commentary

玉璧是春秋战国至汉代最常见的礼仪用器，代表墓
主生前的等级和地位。谷纹是玉璧上最常见的纹
饰，因其像春天谷粒发芽的形状而得名，但其意义
究竟是出于整齐美观，还是有某种宗教意义已不得
而知。谷纹因雕琢技法不同而有不同的表现方式，
这件玉璧上的谷纹采取浮雕方式，即剔除底子，凸
出半球状谷粒状纹饰，显得整齐饱满。

Bi-disc is the most popular jade ritual object symbolizing the rank
and status of the tomb occupant when he or she was alive. Grain
pattern is the most popular design on the jade *bi*-discs, the name
of which is from the pattern's shape like the budding grains. The
relief grain pattern are carved tidy and plump.

点　评
Commentary

这件玉璧上形状如云头一般的谷纹，称为勾连谷纹，实际上是两个谷粒状纹饰尾部相连而形成的。这种样式的谷纹一般流行于春秋晚期至战国早期，到战国晚期时，谷粒之间的尾部完全断开，形成一个个独立的谷粒状纹饰。

The cloud-like grain pattern on this jade *bi*-disc is called "intertwined grain pattern", each unit of which is formed by two grains linked together by the tails. This type of grain pattern was popular in the late Spring-and-Autumn through early Warring States Periods. In the late Warring States Period, the tails of the grain patterns were completely separated and changed into independent grain pattern.

2 谷纹玉璧
Jade *Bi*-disc with Grain Pattern

战国早期礼仪用玉
湖北省荆州市熊家冢墓地出土
直径5.4、孔径2.4、厚0.6厘米

Early Warring States Period
Excavated from Xiongjiazhong Cemetery of Chu State in Jingzhou, Hubei Province
D. (outer) 5.4 cm, D. (inner) 2.4 cm, Th. 0.6 cm

玉质黄褐色，微透明，受沁变红，表面有灰色及黑色沁。扁平体，正圆形，内外缘阴刻由细密的斜线纹组成的轮廓线，两面碾琢勾连谷纹、卷云纹和谷纹。器体有一道断裂痕。

点 评
Commentary

这件玉璧上留下的加工痕迹，是研究玉璧纹饰制作过程的珍贵资料。从痕迹来判断，工匠在雕琢谷纹时，先将璧面四等分，然后逐一加工纹饰。这样制作的优点在于谷纹整齐对称，琢刻便捷。因此，我们可以照此原理将所有谷纹玉璧的纹饰加工过程复原。

The processing traces showed that before engraving the grain pattern, the obverse of the jade *bi*-disc was evenly quartered and the grain patterns in each quartered zone were engraved independently. This way makes the grain patterns tidy and symmetric and easy to engrave.

3 谷纹玉璧
Jade *Bi*-disc with Grain Pattern

战国早期礼仪用玉
湖北省荆州市熊家冢墓地出土
直径8.4、孔径4、厚0.6厘米

Early Warring States Period
Excavated from Xiongjiazhong Cemetery of
Chu State in Jingzhou, Hubei Province
D. (outer) 8.4 cm, D. (inner) 4 cm, Th. 0.6 cm

玉质青绿色，半透明，有灰色、黑色及褐色沁。内外缘有阴刻的轮廓线，正面浅浮雕谷纹、卷云纹、蝌蚪纹。背面一半和正面的纹饰相同，另外一半光素无纹，有阴刻的打稿线和切割痕，为半成品。璧面有裂痕。

点 评
Commentary

这件玉璧上浮雕的谷纹与其他玉璧略有不同，谷粒非半球状或弧形，而似塔尖状，如同螺尾一样，触之有扎手感。这种技法雕琢的谷纹玉璧甚为少见，为古玉收藏界视为珍稀之物。

The grain patterns on this *bi*-disc look like spiral shells with a pointed top. The jade *bi*-discs with grain patterns engraved in this skill are very rare and seen as treasure by the antique jade collectors.

4 谷纹玉璧
Jade *Bi*-disc with Grain Pattern

战国早期礼仪用玉
湖北省荆州市熊家冢墓地出土
直径8.9、孔径3.2、厚0.7厘米

Early Warring States Period
Excavated from Xiongjiazhong Cemetery of
Chu State in Jingzhou, Hubei Province
D. (outer) 8.9 cm, D. (inner) 3.2 cm, Th. 0.7 cm

玉质黄褐色，不透明，有灰色、黑色和黄褐色沁。扁平体，圆形，内外缘有凸起的轮廓线，中间浅浮雕谷纹。

5 谷纹玉璧
Jade *Bi*-disc with Grain Pattern

战国早期礼仪用玉
湖北省荆州市熊家冢墓地出土
直径11、孔径5.3、厚0.6厘米

Early Warring States Period
Excavated from Xiongjiazhong Cemetery of
Chu State in Jingzhou, Hubei Province
D. (outer) 11 cm, D. (inner) 5.3 cm, Th. 0.6 cm

玉质黄绿色，不透明，表面布满灰白色沁。扁平
体，正圆形，内外缘有凸起的轮廓线，中间碾琢
谷纹。

6 谷纹玉璧
Jade Bi-disc with Grain Pattern

战国中期礼仪用玉
湖北省荆州市院墙湾墓地出土
直径9.3、孔径4.5、厚0.6厘米

Middle Warring States Period
Excavated from Yuanqiangwan Cemetery of
Chu State in Jingzhou, Hubei Province
D. (outer) 9.3 cm，D. (inner) 4.5 cm, Th. 0.6 cm

玉质青白色，半透明，温润有光泽，有黑色絮
状斑，大部分受沁变成黑色。扁平体，圆环
形，内外缘有凸起的轮廓线，两面碾琢细密规
整的谷纹。

7 谷纹玉璧
Jade *Bi*-disc with Grain Pattern

战国中期礼仪用玉
湖北省荆州市院墙湾墓地出土
直径3.9、孔径1.6、厚0.5厘米

Middle Warring States Period
Excavated from Yuanqiangwan Cemetery of
Chu State in Jingzhou, Hubei Province
D. (outer) 3.9 cm, D. (inner) 1.6 cm, Th. 0.5 cm

玉质青白色，半透明，有褐色及黑色沁。扁平
体，正圆形，内外缘有凸起的轮廓线，两面碾琢
规整的谷纹。边缘有残损。

8 谷纹玉璧
Jade *Bi*-disc with Grain Pattern

战国中期礼仪用玉
湖北省荆州市院墙湾墓地出土
直径5.4、孔径2.3、厚0.6厘米

Middle Warring States Period
Excavated from Yuanqiangwan Cemetery of
Chu State in Jingzhou, Hubei Provincev
D. (outer) 5.4 cm, D. (inner) 2.3 cm, Th. 0.6 cm

玉质青白色，半透明，夹黑色斑，有褐色沁。扁
平体，正圆形。内外缘有凸起的轮廓线，两面碾
琢谷纹。外缘部分残损。

点 评
Commentary

这件玉璧上的谷纹是以阴刻线的技法制作，形似漩涡，故又称"涡纹"。阴线刻的谷纹常见于玉色较暗的玉璧上，精致及美观程度上不及浮雕的谷纹，大概与这类玉璧多为丧葬用玉有关。

The grain pattern on this jade *bi*-disc is made of sunken lines like whirls, so it is also called "whirl pattern". This pattern is usually applied on the *bi*-discs with dark tints which are mostly used as burial objects. .

9 谷纹玉璧
Jade *Bi*-disc with Grain Pattern

战国晚期礼仪用玉
湖北省荆州市高台墓地出土
直径14、孔径3.8、厚0.5厘米

Late Warring States Period
Excavated from Gaotai Cemetery of
Chu State in Jingzhou, Hubei Province
D. (outer) 14 cm, D. (inner) 3.8 cm, Th. 0.5 cm

玉质青绿色，微透明，夹黑色絮状斑，表面有灰黄色及黑色沁。扁平体，正圆形，内外缘阴刻轮廓线，两面阴刻谷纹。

10 谷纹玉璧
Jade *Bi*-disc with Grain Pattern

战国晚期礼仪用玉
湖北省荆州市高台墓地出土
直径20.4、孔径5.8、厚0.6厘米

Late Warring States Period
Excavated from Gaotai Cemetery of
Chu State in Jingzhou, Hubei Province
D. (outer) 20.4 cm, D. (inner) 5.8 cm, Th. 0.6 cm

玉质深绿色，半透明，表面有红色沁。扁平体，
正圆形，内外缘阴刻轮廓线，两面浅浮雕谷纹。
边缘有残损，中间有一道裂痕。

11 谷纹玉璧
Jade *Bi*-disc with Grain Pattern

战国晚期礼仪用玉
湖北省荆州市谢家桥墓地出土
直径11.9、孔径5.9、厚0.5厘米

Late Warring States Period
Excavated from Xiejiaqiao Cemetery of
Chu State in Jingzhou, Hubei Province
D. (outer) 11.9 cm, D. (inner) 5.9 cm, Th. 0.5 cm

玉质青白色，不透明，受沁严重变成灰白色。扁
体，圆形，内外缘有凸起的轮廓线，中间浅浮雕
细密的谷纹。

点 评
Commentary

勾连云纹是由阴刻的谷纹相互勾连盘绕而成，看上去如同绵延细密的卷云。如果以浮雕方式雕刻谷纹，而以阴刻线将谷粒相连，则称之为勾连谷纹。这种样式是战国流行的纹饰，到汉代逐渐消失。

Intertwined cloud patterns are formed by intaglio grain patterns linked and intertwined together, looking like the tiny and continuous cirrus clouds. If the grain patterns are relief and the lines linking the grains are intaglio, the pattern is called intertwined grain pattern. This pattern was popular in the Warring States Period and vanished in the Han Dynasty.

12 勾连云纹玉璧
Jade *Bi*-disc with Cloud Pattern

战国早期礼仪用玉
湖北省荆州市熊家冢墓地出土
直径9.9、孔径4.4、厚0.7厘米

Early Warring States Period
Excavated from Xiongjiazhong Cemetery of
Chu State in Jingzhou, Hubei Province
D. (outer) 9.9 cm, D. (inner) 4.4 cm, Th. 0.7 cm

玉质青绿色，不透明，有黑色条状及点状斑，表面有灰白色沁。扁平体，正圆形，内外缘有阴刻的轮廓线，两面阴刻勾连云纹。

13 勾连云纹玉璧
Jade *Bi*-disc with Cloud Pattern

战国早期礼仪用玉
湖北省荆州市熊家冢墓地出土
直径17、孔径6.3、厚0.7厘米

Early Warring States Period
Excavated from Xiongjiazhong Cemetery of
Chu State in Jingzhou, Hubei Province
D. (outer) 17 cm, D. (inner) 6.3 cm, Th. 0.7 cm

玉质青绿色，微透明，表面布满了灰白色沁，也
有少量的黑色沁。扁平体，圆形，内外缘有阴
刻的轮廓线，纹饰分为三区，内、外两区各有两
周由交错的网格纹组成的纹饰，中间阴刻勾连云
纹。由于切割原因，导致玉璧的厚薄不均匀。

14 勾连云纹玉璧
Jade *Bi*-disc with Cloud Pattern

战国早期礼仪用玉
湖北省荆州市熊家冢墓地出土
直径9.7、孔径3.8、厚0.5厘米

Early Warring States Period
Excavated from Xiongjiazhong Cemetery of
Chu State in Jingzhou, Hubei Province
D. (outer) 9.7 cm, D. (inner) 3.8 cm, Th. 0.5 cm

玉质黄绿色，微透明，有红褐色沁，表面受沁呈
灰白色。扁平体，正圆形。内外缘有阴刻的轮廓
线，中间阴刻勾连云纹。有切割痕和裂痕。

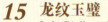

15 龙纹玉璧
Jade *Bi*-disc with Dragon Pattern

战国晚期礼仪用玉
湖北省荆州市高台墓地出土
直径21.1、孔径4.4、厚0.55厘米

Late Warring States Period
Excavated from Gaotai Cemetery of
Chu State in Jingzhou, Hubei Province
D. (outer) 21.1 cm, D. (inner) 4.4 cm, Th. 0.55 cm

玉质青绿色，半透明。有黑色斑及少量褐色沁。
扁平体，正圆形，内外缘阴刻轮廓线，中间有
一圈绚索纹将纹饰分为两区。外区阴刻四组一首
双身的龙纹。龙长卷角，圆眼，卷鼻，躬身，卷
尾。内区浅浮雕规则的谷纹，谷纹之间有直线状
擦痕。

16 龙纹玉璧
Jade *Bi*-disc with Dragon Pattern

战国晚期礼仪用玉
湖北省荆州市高台墓地出土
直径16.1、孔径4.9、厚0.6厘米

Late Warring States Period
Excavated from Gaotai Cemetery of
Chu State in Jingzhou, Hubei Province
D. (outer) 16.1 cm, D. (inner) 4.9 cm, Th. 0.6 cm

玉质青色，微透明，已受沁变成灰黄色。扁平
体，正圆形，内外缘阴刻轮廓线，中间有一圈绚
索纹将纹饰分为两区，外区有三组纹饰，各组之
间由两条阴刻线的条状带分隔。每组阴刻一首双
身的龙纹。龙头左右各有一个长角伸出。梭形
眼，卷鼻，躬身，卷尾。内区阴刻谷纹。两面纹
饰相同。

点 评
Commentary

这种有双周纹饰带的玉璧，一般玉料为青绿色，
雕工较粗率，多做丧葬用玉，民间收藏界称之为
"祭坑玉"。战国晚期至汉代，等级较高的墓葬
中往往成组放置在墓主的前胸和后背上，应该是
丧葬等级观念的反映。

This kind of jade *bi*-discs with double rim decorative bands are
usually made of bluish-green raw materials and in crude skill, and
they are mostly used as funeral objects. In the late Warring States
Period through the Han Dynasty, this kind of jade *bi*-discs were
usually put in groups on the chest or the back of the occupants
of the high-ranking tombs, showing the hierarchical views in the
burial customs.

17 透雕双龙纹玉璧

Jade *Bi*-disc with Double Dragons Pattern in Openwork

战国早期礼仪用玉
湖北省荆州市熊家冢墓地出土
通长9.4、璧径5.6、孔径2.4、厚0.5厘米

Early Warring States Period
Excavated from Xiongjiazhong Cemetery of
Chu State in Jingzhou, Hubei Province
Overall L. 9.4 cm, D. (outer) 5.6 cm, D. (inner) 2.4 cm,
Th. 0.5 cm

玉质黄白色，半透明，有红褐色及灰色沁。璧扁平体，正圆形，内外缘阴刻轮廓线，中间浅浮雕勾连云纹及蝌蚪纹，两面纹饰相同。两侧透雕背向而立的龙，与璧外缘相连。龙圆眼，回首，躬身，卷尾，一足前伸。龙身浅浮雕谷纹，龙足阴刻斜线纹。

点 评
Commentary

所谓"蝌蚪纹",是指璧面纹饰外侧边缘有四个对称分布的单体谷纹。这种谷纹拖着长直且宽大的尾,形同蝌蚪一般。蝌蚪纹亦称"卧蚕纹",也像一条伏卧的蚕一样。它是战国早期流行的谷纹样式。

Tadpole pattern refers to the four isolated grain patterns arranged symmetrically on the outer edge of the pattern zone of the jade *bi*-disc. The grain pattern with long, straight and wide tail looks like a tadpole or a prone silkworm, so it is also called as "prone silkworm pattern." It is the type of grain patterns popular in early Warring States Period.

18 透雕龙纹双联玉璧
Jade Joined Double *Bi*-discs with Double Dragons
Pattern in Openwork

战国早期礼仪用玉
湖北省荆州市熊家冢墓地出土
通长4.2、璧径2.1、孔径0.75、厚0.6厘米

Early Warring States Period
Excavated from Xiongjiazhong Cemetery of
Chu State in Jingzhou, Hubei Province
Overall L. 4.2 cm, D. (outer) 2.1 cm, D. (inner) 0.75 cm,
Th. 0.6 cm

玉质黄绿色，不透明，受沁大部分变成灰白色。
透雕连体两龙，勾喙，独角向内翻卷，身下透雕
两个相连的素面玉璧。

点评
Commentary

蟠虺纹是春秋时期的代表性纹饰，战国早期仍在流行。蟠虺是指盘绕的小龙，蟠虺纹是由若干侧面龙首组成的细密丰满的纹饰。"S"纹和卷云纹是构成蟠虺纹的主要纹饰，它们都可以被视作谷纹的变形组合体。它们的阴刻线条较宽，颇有西周"斜刀工"的韵味。值得注意的是，"S"纹的纹道中有一条斜向的分割线，而卷云纹却没有，这说明"S"纹是由两个谷纹从反方向错尾雕成的。

Coiled dragon design was the representative decorative design in the Spring-and-Autumn Period and still popular in the early Warring-States Period. The coiled dragon design is close and plump decorative design consisting of profiled dragon heads; the main parts forming the coiled dragon design are S-shaped curves and cirrus cloud patterns, both of which can be seen as the stylized components of grain patterns.

19　蟠虺纹玉璧
Jade *Bi*-disc with Coiled Dragon Pattern

战国早期礼仪用玉
湖北省荆州市熊家冢墓地出土
直径15.3、孔径6.3、厚0.8厘米

Early Warring States Period
Excavated from Xiongjiazhong Cemetery of
Chu State in Jingzhou, Hubei Province
D. (outer)　15.3 cm, D. (inner)　6.3 cm, Th. 0.8 cm

玉质青绿色，微透明，表面布满了灰黄色及黑色夹杂的沁斑。扁平体，正圆形，内外缘阴刻轮廓线。两面纹饰分三区，内外两区都阴刻由连续三角纹、卷云纹、网格纹组成的纹饰，中间阴刻四组蟠虺纹，都是由阴刻的"S"纹、卷云纹、圆圈纹及网格纹组成。璧中间有一道明显的切割痕迹。

20 蟠虺纹玉璧
Jade *Bi*-disc with Coiled Dragon Pattern

战国早期礼仪用玉
湖北省荆州市熊家冢墓地出土
直径9、孔径4.2、厚0.5厘米

Early Warring States Period
Excavated from Xiongjiazhong Cemetery of
Chu State in Jingzhou, Hubei Province
D. (outer) 9 cm, D. (inner) 4.2 cm, Th. 0.5 cm

玉质青绿色，微透明，有红褐色沁，表面受沁变
成灰白色。扁平体，正圆形。内外缘有阴刻的轮
廓线，中间阴刻四组蟠虺纹。有切割痕。两面纹
饰相同。

21　蟠虺纹玉璧
Jade *Bi*-disc with Coiled Dragon Pattern

战国早期礼仪用玉
湖北省荆州市熊家冢墓地出土
直径9.6、孔径4.6、厚0.6厘米

Early Warring States Period
Excavated from Xiongjiazhong Cemetery of
Chu State in Jingzhou, Hubei Province
D. (outer) 9.6 cm, D. (inner) 4.6 cm, Th. 0.6 cm

玉质黄绿色，微透明，有红褐色沁，表面受沁变
成灰白色。扁平体，正圆形。内外缘有阴刻的轮
廓线，中间阴刻四组蟠虺纹。

点 评
Commentary

像这样透雕精美的玉器，一直是古玉收藏界收藏的重点。透雕工艺发展到战国和汉代达到了顶峰，构图严谨对称，具有剪纸般的效果，纹饰精美，线条流畅，这与制玉工具的进步有直接的关系。战国时期，铁制工具代替了青铜工具，铁制工具具有硬度高不易磨损、可锻打出细薄锐利的砣子、原料易得且成本低等特点，因此从战国时期直到近代制玉工具都是铁制的。

The jades with such exquisite openwork designs are the key pursuit targets of antique jade collectors. Openwork technique developed to its climax in the Warring-States Period and the Han Dynasty, the motifs are cautiously organized and symmetric with effects of paper cut, the designs are fine and the lines are smooth, all of which are directly related to the progresses of the jade work tools.

22 透雕蟠螭纹玉璧
Jade *Bi*-disc with Coiled Dragon Pattern in Openwork

战国早期礼仪用玉
湖北省荆州市熊家冢墓地出土
直径10.5、孔径4、厚0.4厘米

Early Warring States Period
Excavated from Xiongjiazhong Cemetery of
Chu State in Jingzhou, Hubei Province
D. (outer) 10.5 cm, D. (inner) 4 cm, Th. 0.4 cm

玉质青白色，半透明，有灰褐、黑、灰白色沁。
造型由内外两环和环间的透雕蟠螭纹组成。外环
阴刻两道轮廓线，其间刻云纹。内环阴刻两道轮
廓线，其间刻谷纹、勾连纹。两环之间透雕蟠螭
八条，分为四组，两两相缠，曲身卷尾，腹部有
一足，螭首刻双目、双角纹，身躯刻斜线纹。局
部残断。

23 玉璧
Jade *Bi*-disc

战国早期礼仪用玉
湖北省荆州市熊家冢墓地出土
直径6、孔径2.8、厚0.5厘米

Early Warring States Period
Excavated from Xiongjiazhong Cemetery of
Chu State in Jingzhou, Hubei Province
D. (outer) 6 cm, D. (inner) 2.8 cm, Th. 0.5 cm

玉质青绿色，微透明，有灰色沁。扁平体，正圆
形，素面无纹，边缘略有残。

24　玉璧
Jade *Bi*-disc

战国早期礼仪用玉
湖北省荆州市熊家冢墓地出土
直径9.7、孔径3.5、厚0.5厘米

Early Warring States Period
Excavated from Xiongjiazhong Cemetery of
Chu State in Jingzhou, Hubei Province
D. (outer)　9.7 cm, D. (inner)　3.5 cm, Th. 0.5 cm

玉质黄绿色，不透明，有灰白色沁。扁平体，正
圆形。平素无纹。有切割痕。

点 评
Commentary

这种滑石璧主要流行于湖北、湖南等楚国疆域内，应该是具有楚国玉器特点的器物，西汉早期的墓里仍有出土。它的式样很显然是仿谷纹玉璧，是一种专为随葬所制作的玉器替代品。

The *bi*-discs made of talc are mainly distributed in present-day Hubei and Hunan, which were in the domain of the Chu State in the Warring-States Period, so it should have belonged to the Chu jade system. In tombs of the early Western Han Dynasty, talc *bi*-discs could also be unearthed. Obviously, talc *bi*-disc is the imitation of the jade *bi*-discs with grain pattern specially made as funeral objects instead of the real jade *bi*-discs.

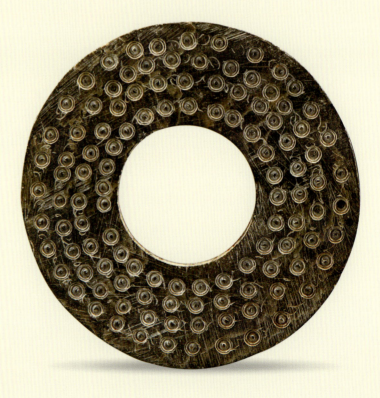

25 圆涡纹石璧
Soapstone *Bi*-disc with Whirlpool Pattern

战国时期礼仪用玉
湖北省荆州市鸡公山墓地出土
直径12.2、孔径5、厚0.6厘米

Warring States Period
Excavated from Jigongshan Cemetery of
Chu State in Jingzhou, Hubei Province
D. (outer) 12.2 cm, D. (inner) 5 cm, Th. 0.6 cm

滑石质，青灰色，不透明。扁平体，正圆形，璧厚薄不均，两面浅浮雕圆涡纹。

26 谷纹玉环
Jade Ring with Grain Pattern

战国早期礼仪用玉
湖北省荆州市熊家冢墓地出土
直径7.2、孔径3.9、厚0.6厘米

Early Warring States Period
Excavated from Xiongjiazhong Cemetery of
Chu State in Jingzhou, Hubei Province
D. (outer) 7.2 cm, D. (inner) 3.9 cm, Th. 0.6 cm

玉质黄绿色，微透明，夹黑色条状斑，有黄褐色
及黑色沁。扁平体，正圆形，内外缘阴刻轮廓
线，两面碾琢谷纹及蝌蚪纹。

27 谷纹玉环
Jade Ring with Grain Pattern

战国早期礼仪用玉
湖北省荆州市熊家冢墓地出土
直径7.1、孔径4、厚0.6厘米

Early Warring States Period
Excavated from Xiongjiazhong Cemetery of
Chu State in Jingzhou, Hubei Province
D. (outer) 7.1 cm, D. (inner) 4 cm, Th. 0.6 cm

玉质青绿色，不透明，有灰白色及黑褐色沁。扁
平体，正圆形。内外缘有凸起的轮廓线，中间碾
琢谷纹。部分有残损。

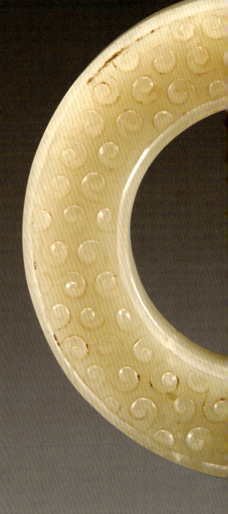

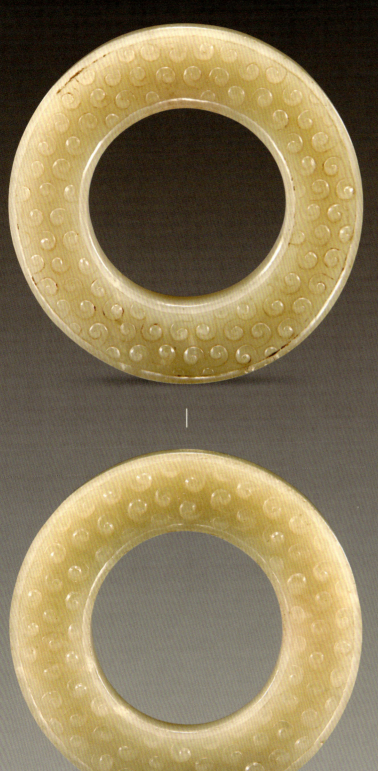

28 谷纹玉环
Jade Ring with Grain Pattern

战国中期礼仪用玉
湖北省荆州市院墙湾墓地出土
直径5.4、孔径3、厚0.6厘米

Middle Warring States Period
Excavated from Yuanqiangwan Cemetery of
Chu State in Jingzhou, Hubei Province
D. (outer) 5.4 cm, D. (inner) 3 cm, Th. 0.6 cm

玉质乳白色，细腻致密，半透明。扁平体，圆环
形。内外缘有凸起轮廓线，两面碾琢规整的谷纹。

（正）

29　谷纹玉环
Jade Ring with Grain Pattern

战国中期礼仪用玉
湖北省荆州市院墙湾墓地出土
直径11.6、孔径7、厚0.7厘米

Middle Warring States Period
Excavated from Yuanqiangwan Cemetery of
Chu State in Jingzhou, Hubei Province
D. (outer) 11.6 cm, D. (inner) 7 cm, Th. 0.7 cm

玉质碧绿色，半透明，温润，有光泽，有少量黑
色点状斑。扁平体，圆环形，内外缘有凸起轮廓
线，两面碾琢谷纹。

（背）

30 绞丝纹玉环
Jade Rings with Twisting Rope Pattern (3 pieces)

战国中期玉佩饰
湖北省荆州市江陵雨台山墓地出土
上：外径3.9、内径2.2、厚0.8厘米
左：外径3.1、内径1.8、厚0.5厘米
右：外径3.1、内径1.8、厚0.5厘米

Middle Warring States Period
Excavated from Yutaishan Cemetery of Chu State in Jiangling,
Jingzhou, Hubei Province
Above: D. (outer) 3.9cm, D. (inner) 2.2cm, Th.0.8cm
Left: D. (outer) 3.1cm, D. (inner) 1.8cm, Th.0.5cm
Right: D. (outer) 3.1 cm, D. (inner) 1.8 cm, Th. 0.5 cm

3件，玉质青白色，微透明，有灰白色和橘黄色
沁。圆环状，表面阴线雕琢细密的绞丝纹。

点　评
Commentary

所谓"绞丝纹"，形象地说就是用一条细绳子斜向缠绕在玉镯子上，只不过这条绳子循环往复没有尽头。据说这种现象在数学上叫"阿基米德螺线"，亦称"等速螺线"，是古希腊伟大的数学家阿基米德发现的。有趣的是，阿基米德生活的时代正是中国的战国时期，也就是这件绞丝纹玉环制作的时代。

In mathematics, the twisting rope pattern is called "Archimedean spiral" or "arithmetic spiral", because in the West, it was discovered by Archimedes, a great mathematician of ancient Greece. It is interesting that the period when Archimedes was living was just the Warring-States Period in China, and also the time when this jade ring with twisting rope pattern was made.

31 蟠虺纹玉环
Jade Ring with Coiled Dragon Pattern

战国早期礼仪用玉
湖北省荆州市熊家冢墓地出土
直径10.2、孔径5.7、厚0.6厘米

Early Warring States Period
Excavated from Xiongjiazhong Cemetery of
Chu State in Jingzhou, Hubei Province
D. (outer) 10.2 cm, D. (inner) 5.7 cm, Th. 0.6 cm

玉质黄绿色，微透明，有黑色条状斑，夹灰白色
及褐色沁。扁平体，正圆形，内外缘都阴刻轮
廓线。两面阴刻蟠虺纹，共五组，都是由阴刻的
"S"形纹、卷云纹、圆圈纹及网格纹组成。

32 蟠虺纹玉环
Jade Ring with Coiled Dragon Pattern

战国早期礼仪用玉
湖北省荆州市熊家冢墓地出土
直径9、孔径4.9、厚0.6厘米

Early Warring States Period
Excavated from Xiongjiazhong Cemetery of
Chu State in Jingzhou, Hubei Province
D. (outer) 9 cm, D. (inner) 4.9 cm, Th. 0.6 cm

玉质黄绿色，不透明，布满了灰白色沁。扁平体，
正圆形。内外缘有阴刻的轮廓线，两面共五组由阴
刻的"S"形纹、卷云纹及网格纹组成的蟠虺纹。

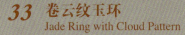

33 卷云纹玉环
Jade Ring with Cloud Pattern

战国早期礼仪用玉
湖北省荆州市熊家冢墓地出土
直径5.8、孔径3.3、厚0.5厘米

Early Warring States Period
Excavated from Xiongjiazhong Cemetery of
Chu State in Jingzhou, Hubei Province
D. (outer) 5.8 cm, D. (inner) 3.3 cm, Th. 0.5 cm

玉质青绿色，半透明，有黑褐色沁。扁平体，正
圆形，内外缘有阴刻的轮廓线，两面共八组由阴
刻的卷云纹、羽冠状网格纹组成的纹饰。

34 卷云纹玉环
Jade Ring with Cloud Pattern

战国中期礼仪用玉
湖北省荆州市院墙湾墓地出土
直径6.1、孔径5.1、厚0.5厘米

Middle Warring States Period
Excavated from Yuanqiangwan Cemetery of
Chu State in Jingzhou, Hubei Province
D. (outer) 6.1 cm, D. (inner) 5.1 cm, Th. 0.5 cm

玉质黄白色，半透明，有红褐色沁。扁平体，圆
环形。内外缘阴刻轮廓线，两面纹饰稍有不同，
正面阴刻勾连云纹，反面阴刻卷云纹。

35 卷云纹玉环
Jade Ring with Cloud Pattern

战国时期礼仪用玉
湖北省荆州市黄山墓地出土
直径6.4、孔径3.8、厚0.4厘米

Warring States Period
Excavated from Huangshan Cemetery of
Chu State in Jingzhou, Hubei Province
D. (outer) 6.4 cm, D. (inner) 3.8 cm, Th. 0.4 cm

玉质红褐色，微透明。扁平体，圆环形，内外缘
阴刻轮廓线，两面饰卷云纹及网格纹。

点 评
Commentary

这件玉环上的卷云纹，线条婉转流畅，网格纹内线条细密整齐，颇有"游丝毛雕"的韵味（古玩行形容战汉玉器细腻的阴刻纹饰用语）。阴刻线越细，说明砣子的砣口越薄越锋利，这与铁砣的使用有直接关系，因为铁可以反复锻打，形成坚硬而锋利的砣口。

The cloud pattern on this jade ring is carved with smooth and tender lines, and the lines of the check board pattern are thin, close and tidy, all of which showed that the emery wheel used for carving the patterns was thin and sharp; this hinted that iron wheel had been applied because only the iron wheel can be forged into this hard and sharp edge.

36 勾连云纹玉环
Jade Ring with Cloud Pattern

战国早期礼仪用玉
湖北省荆州市熊家冢墓地出土
直径12.1、孔径6.8、厚0.6厘米

Early Warring States Period
Excavated from Xiongjiazhong Cemetery of
Chu State in Jingzhou, Hubei Province
D. (outer) 12.1 cm, D. (inner) 6.8 cm, Th. 0.6 cm

玉质青绿色，不透明，表面有灰白色及少量黄褐
色沁。扁平体，正圆形，内外缘有阴刻轮廓线，
两面纹饰分三区，内、外两区都阴刻连续三角
纹、卷云纹，中间阴刻谷纹、云纹及勾连云纹。

37 "S"形云纹玉环
Jade Ring with S-shaped Cloud Pattern

战国中期礼仪用玉
湖北省荆州市江陵凤凰山墓地出土
直径9.4、孔径5.1、厚0.6厘米

Middle Warring States Period
Excavated from Fenghuangshan Cemetery of
Chu State in Jiangling, Jingzhou, Hubei Province
D. (outer) 9.4 cm, D. (inner) 5.1 cm, Th. 0.6 cm

玉质青白色，不透明，有黑色沁。扁平体、圆环
形。外缘有阴刻的轮廓线，中间阴刻四组由"S"
形云纹及网格纹组成的纹饰。

38 龙纹玉环
Jade Ring with Dragon Pattern

战国时期玉佩饰
湖北省荆州市岳桥印合墓地出土
直径2.1、孔径0.7、厚0.5厘米

Warring States Period
Excavated from Yueqiaoyintai Cemetery of
Chu State in Jingzhou, Hubei Province
D. (outer) 2.1 cm, D. (inner) 0.7 cm, Th. 0.5 cm

玉质乳白色，半透明，有黄褐色沁。圆环状，阴
刻三组纹饰，每组都是由一对相向的龙纹组成。
璧面上有一孔，边缘亦有钻孔痕迹。

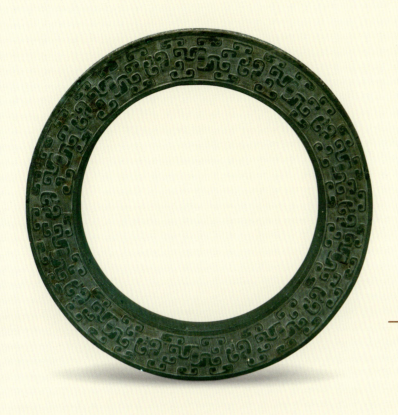

39 蟠虺纹琉璃环
Glass Ring with Coiled Dragon Pattern

战国晚期礼仪用玉
湖北省荆州市谢家桥墓地出土
直径10.8厘米，孔径7.6厘米，厚0.9厘米

Late Warring States Period
Excavated from Xiejiaqiao Cemetery of
Chu State in Jingzhou, Hubei Province
D. (outer) 10.8 cm, D. (inner) 7.6 cm, Th. 0.9 cm

蓝色琉璃，有气泡，半透明。内外缘有凸起的轮
廓线，中间浅浮雕十组蟠虺纹及卷云纹，两面纹
饰相同。璧的外侧面也浅浮雕细密的蟠虺纹。

点评
Commentary

这件琉璃环堪称早期玻璃器的精品，不但质地纯
净，透明度高，而且满饰细密的蟠虺纹，相当精
致。中国早期的玻璃器，"蜻蜓眼"琉璃珠，一
般认为是从西亚输入的，因为当时在西亚以及欧
洲地中海沿岸也大量流行这种珠子，但是这种蟠
虺纹环的造型是中国特有的，因此这件琉璃环应
该是中国本土的产物，代表了当时玻璃器生产的
最高水平。

It is generally believed that the earliest glass wares in China
were imported from the West Asia, but the shaping and the fine
coiled dragon design of this glass ring are all peculiar to China, so
this glass ring would be local product of China representing the
highest level of Chinese glass industry at that time.

点 评
Commentary

这种内厚外薄的玛瑙环，是与带钩组合使用的束带用具，流行于战国时期，也称"带环"。带环一侧拴系腰带，对应的另一侧扣入带钩的带首，达到束带的目的。鸡血玛瑙是玛瑙中比较珍贵的品种，红色部分似流动的鸡血，出土也比较少。

This kind of agate ring with thicker inner rim and thinner outer rim is a belt fitting assembled with a belt hook, so it was also called "belt ring" in the WarringStates Period. The "blood agate" is valuable type of agate, the red part of which looks like flowing blood, and the artworks made of this type of agate are rarely seen in burials.

40　鸡血玛瑙环
Chalcedony Rings (2 pieces)

战国晚期玛瑙佩饰
湖北省荆州市天星观墓地出土
直径5.5、孔径2.9厘米

Late Warring States Period
Excavated from Tianxingguan Cemetery of
Chu State in Jingzhou, Hubei Province
D. (outer) 5.5 cm, D. (inner) 2.9 cm

2件，玛瑙质，有白色及鸡血红两种颜色。内缘较厚，外缘较薄，呈刀状。抛光较亮，有断裂痕。

41 玛瑙环
Chalcedony Ring

战国时期玛瑙佩饰
湖北省荆州市枣林岗墓地出土
直径7.5、孔径4.4、厚1厘米

Warring States Period
Excavated from Zaolingang Cemetery of
Chu State in Jingzhou, Hubei Province
D. (outer) 7.5 cm, D. (inner) 4.4 cm, Th. 1 cm

乳白色玛瑙质，透明，有白色絮状斑。圆环状，
内缘较厚，外缘较薄，呈刃状。内缘有宽0.6厘米
的小平台。

42 玛瑙环
Chalcedony Ring

战国晚期玛瑙佩饰
湖北省荆州市天星观墓地出土
直径7.9、孔径4.8、厚1.1厘米

Late Warring States Period
Excavated from Tianxingguan Cemetery of
Chu State in Jingzhou, Hubei Province
D. (outer) 7.9 cm, D. (inner) 4.8 cm, Th. 1.1 cm

白色玛瑙质，透明，有黄色条状斑。圆环状，内
缘较厚，外缘较薄，呈刃状。内缘有宽0.4厘米的
小平台。边缘有残损。

43 水晶环
Rock Crystal Ring

战国早期礼仪用玉
湖北省荆州市熊家冢墓地出土
高1.8、直径3.1、孔径2.1、厚0.8厘米

Early Warring States Period
Excavated from Xiongjiazhong Cemetery of
Chu State in Jingzhou, Hubei Province
H. 1.8 cm, D. (outer) 3.1 cm, D. (inner) 2.1 cm, Th. 0.8 cm

白色透明水晶。圆柱形，中空，双面钻孔，内壁中
间有一道凸棱。环的左右两侧各有一处断裂痕。

44 谷纹玉璜

Jade *Huang*-semicircular Pendant with Grain
Pattern

战国早期礼仪用玉
湖北省荆州市熊家冢墓地出土
长15.5、宽2.9、厚0.7厘米

Early Warring States Period
Excavated from Xiongjiazhong Cemetery of
Chu State in Jingzhou, Hubei Province
L. 15.5 cm, W. 2.9 cm, Th. 0.7 cm

玉质黄绿色，不透明，受沁变成灰黑色。扁平
体，扇形。边缘雕刻出对称的扉棱。内外缘有阴
刻的轮廓线，两端雕出简化龙首，有胡须及眼
睛，饰减地谷纹。璜的两面中间阴刻出扇形图
案，图案的四条边缘阴刻勾连云纹。扇形图案内
饰减地谷纹。顶端有一单面钻圆孔。

45 谷纹玉璜
A Pair of Jade *Huang*-semicircular Pendants with Grain Pattern

战国中期礼仪用玉
湖北省荆州市院墙湾墓地出土
左：长15.9、宽2.5、厚0.6厘米
右：长15.9、宽2.6、厚0.6厘米

Middle Warring States Period
Excavated from Yuanqiangwan Cemetery of
Chu State in Jingzhou, Hubei Province
Left: L. 15.9 cm, W. 2.5 cm, Th. 0.6 cm
Right: L. 15.9 cm, W. 2.6 cm, Th. 0.6 cm

一对，玉质青绿色，微透明，边缘有黑褐色沁。
扁平体，扇形，边缘雕刻出对称的扉棱，外缘有
阴刻的轮廓线，璜体碾琢勾连谷纹。顶端有一圆
穿孔。

46 谷纹玉璜
A Pair of Jade *Huang*-semicircular Pendants with
Grain Pattern

战国中期礼仪用玉
湖北省荆州市院墙湾墓地出土
均长9.9、宽2.3、厚0.4厘米

Middle Warring States Period
Excavated from Yuanqiangwan Cemetery of
Chu State in Jingzhou, Hubei Province
L. 9.9 cm, W. 2.3 cm, Th. 0.4 cm (both)

一对，玉质青绿色，半透明，夹黑色斑，有红褐
色沁。扁平体，扇形。两侧雕刻出对称的扉棱，
外缘有阴刻的轮廓线，中间阴刻谷纹，中部及左
侧有一圆穿孔。

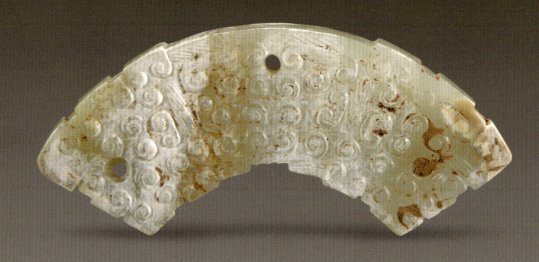

47 **谷纹玉璜**
Jade *Huang*-semicircular Pendant with Grain
Pattern

战国时期礼仪用玉
湖北省荆州市紫荆砖瓦厂墓地出土
长6.8、宽2.1、厚0.6厘米

Warring States Period
Excavated from Zijingzhuanwachang Cemetery of
Chu State in Jingzhou, Hubei Province
L. 6.8 cm, W. 2.1 cm, Th. 0.6 cm

玉质青白色，半透明，有黄褐色沁。扁平体，扇形。两侧雕刻出对称的扉棱，中间浅浮雕四道绚索纹组成一个扇面，中间及两侧浅浮雕勾连谷纹及蝌蚪纹。顶端及两侧各有一个圆穿孔。两面纹饰相同。

48 蟠虺纹玉璜

Jade *Huang*-semicircular Pendant with Coiled
Dragon Pattern

战国早期礼仪用玉
湖北省荆州市熊家冢墓地出土
长12.6、宽2.7、厚0.5厘米

Early Warring States Period
Excavated from Xiongjiazhong Cemetery of
Chu State in Jingzhou, Hubei Province
L. 12.6 cm, W. 2.7 cm, Th. 0.5 cm

玉质黄白色，半透明，有橘黄色及黑色沁。扁平
体，扇形，一端下缘略有残。两侧雕刻出对称的
扉棱，外缘有阴刻的轮廓线。璜的左右两侧阴刻
蟠虺纹，由对称的龙首以及"S"形纹、勾连云纹
和网格纹组成。顶端有一圆穿孔。

49 蟠虺纹玉璜
Jade *Huang*-semicircular Pendant with Coiled Dragon Pattern

战国早期礼仪用玉
湖北省荆州市熊家冢墓地出土
长16.1、宽2.9、厚0.4厘米

Early Warring States Period
Excavated from Xiongjiazhong Cemetery of
Chu State in Jingzhou, Hubei Province
L. 16.1 cm, W. 2.9 cm, Th. 0.4 cm

玉质黄绿色，不透明，受沁严重变成灰白色。扁平体，扇形。两侧雕刻出对称的扉棱，璜体左右两侧阴刻对称的蟠虺纹、交叉"S"形纹及网格纹。两面纹饰相同。有切割痕，顶端有一圆穿孔。

点 评
Commentary

玉璜上的切割痕明显是直片形锯切割的痕迹。古代解玉工具有两种，即直片形锯（条形锯）和线锯（拉丝锯）两种。前者像今天的锯条一样，切割时做水平往复运动，留下的痕迹是直线形的；线锯是像线绳一样的软质工具，在切割时做半圆形或弧形运动，留下的痕迹是细密的同心圆状弧形的。这件玉璜上留下来的切割痕迹非常直，说明琢玉工具在使用时稳定性相当好。

The cutting traces left on this *huang*-semicircular pendant are clearly made by band saw. Like modern band saw, the saw made repeating backward and forward movement when cutting, so the traces it left are straight. The cutting traces on this *huang* are very straight, showing that the jade processing mechanism had very good stability in use.

50 蟠虺纹玉璜

Jade *Huang*-semicircular Pendant with Coiled
Dragon Pattern

战国早期礼仪用玉
湖北省荆州市熊家冢墓地出土
长15、宽2.2、厚0.4厘米

Early Warring States Period
Excavated from Xiongjiazhong Cemetery of
Chu State in Jingzhou, Hubei Province
L. 15 cm, W. 2.2 cm, Th. 0.4 cm

玉质青白色，微透明，受沁严重变成灰白色。扁
平体，扇形。两侧雕刻出对称的扉棱，璜的左右
两侧雕刻对称的三组蟠虺纹及网格纹。顶端有一
圆穿孔。

51 透雕龙凤虺纹玉璜

Jade *Huang*-semicircular Pendant with Dragon and Phoenix Pattern in Openwork

战国早期礼仪用玉
湖北省荆州市熊家冢墓地出土
长13、宽7.2、厚0.6厘米

Early Warring States Period
Excavated from Xiongjiazhong Cemetery of Chu State in Jingzhou, Hubei Province
L. 13 cm, W. 7.2 cm, Th. 0.6 cm

玉质青白色，半透明，有红褐、灰白色沁。扁平体，扇形。一端缺失约三分之一，断口被打磨光滑。璜体正中有一穿孔，图案以此为中轴左右对称展开，透雕凤、虺、龙等动物的轮廓。两凤相背而立，作展翅状。虺状如蛇，尾卷如钩。龙作回首状，躯体盘旋如"8"字形。

点 评
Commentary

这件玉璜有一端缺失，乍一看图案有些混乱，但如果懂得战国玉器构图原则，就很容易理解玉器图案。玉璜属于平衡佩戴的玉器，所以纹饰图案结构一定是中轴对称式，也就是说中轴左右的纹饰是一样的。这件玉璜的中轴就是那个圆穿孔（供系绳佩戴之用），尽管缺失的那部分永远无法复原了，但我们至少可以根据完整的部分在纸上把缺失的图案画出来。

The jade *huang*-semicircular pendant is worn in balance, so the decorative motifs on it are symmetric about a central axis. The central axis of this *huang* is the circular perforation (for strings to go through to hang or bear), so we can restore the missing part based on the extant part.

52 勾连云纹玉璜
Jade *Huang*-semicircular Pendant with Cloud
Pattern

战国早期礼仪用玉
湖北省荆州市熊家冢墓地出土
长15.4、宽2.6、厚0.6厘米

Early Warring States Period
Excavated from Xiongjiazhong Cemetery of
Chu State in Jingzhou, Hubei Province
L. 15.4 cm, W. 2.6 cm, Th. 0.6 cm

玉质青绿色，半透明，有红褐色及灰白色沁。扁平
体，扇形，两侧有对称的扉棱。内外缘有阴刻的轮
廓线，中间阴刻勾连云纹。顶端有一圆穿孔。

53 勾连云纹玉璜
A Pair of Jade *Huang*-semicircular Pendants with Cloud Pattern

战国早期礼仪用玉
湖北省荆州市熊家冢墓地出土
左：长13.7、宽2.5、厚0.6厘米
右：长14.1、宽2.5、厚0.7厘米

Early Warring States Period
Excavated from Xiongjiazhong Cemetery of
Chu State in Jingzhou, Hubei Province
Left: L. 13.7 cm, W. 2.5 cm, Th. 0.6 cm
Right: L. 14.1 cm, W. 2.5 cm, Th. 0.7 cm

一对，玉质青绿色，半透明，夹黑色点状斑，有
灰白色及橘黄色沁。扁平体，扇形。两侧雕刻出
对称的扉棱，外缘有阴刻的轮廓线。璜体阴刻勾
连云纹、"S"形纹及网格纹，扇面左右两侧纹饰
对称。顶端有一圆穿孔。

54 勾连云纹玉璜
A Pair of Jade *Huang*-semicircular Pendants with Cloud Pattern

战国晚期礼仪用玉
湖北省荆州市谢家桥墓地出土
左：长17.3、宽3.1、厚0.4厘米
右：长17.1、宽3、厚0.5厘米

Late Warring States Period
Excavated from Xiejiaqiao Cemetery of
Chu State in Jingzhou, Hubei Province
Left: L. 17.3 cm, W. 3.1 cm, Th. 0.4 cm
Right: L. 17.1 cm, W. 3 cm, Th. 0.5 cm

一对，玉质青绿色，微透明，夹黑色点状斑，边缘有少量黄褐色沁。扁平体，扇形，内外缘有阴刻的轮廓线，四周有扉棱，顶端有一圆穿孔，中间阴刻勾连云纹。下面的玉璜边缘有裂痕。

55 "S"形云纹玉璜

Jade *Huang*-semicircular Pendant with S-shaped
Cloud Pattern

战国早期礼仪用玉
湖北省荆州市熊家冢墓地出土
长13.3、宽3、厚0.6厘米

Early Warring States Period
Excavated from Xiongjiazhong Cemetery of
Chu State in Jingzhou, Hubei Province
L. 13.3 cm, W. 3 cm, Th. 0.6 cm

玉质青绿色，半透明，夹黑色点状斑。扁平体，
半环形。边缘雕刻出对称的扉棱，内外缘有阴刻的
轮廓线。璜面左右阴刻对称的单体和交叉"S"形
云纹，以及形态各异的网格纹。顶端有一圆穿孔。

56 几何形云纹玉璜
Jade *Huang*-semicircular Pendant with Cloud Pattern

春秋晚期礼仪用玉
湖北省荆州市秦家山墓地出土
长6.5、宽1.8、厚0.4厘米

Late Spring and Autumn Period
Excavated from Qinjiashan Cemetery of
Chu State in Jingzhou, Hubei Province
L. 6.5 cm, W. 1.8 cm, Th. 0.4 cm

玉质青白色，半透明，夹黑色斑，边缘有糖色沁。
扁平体，扇形。两端各有一穿孔。边缘有阴刻的轮
廓线，中间阴刻几何形云纹。两面纹饰相同。

点 评
Commentary

几何形云纹是指线条转折近直角形，有些像云雷
纹的纹饰。这种纹饰特征有秦式玉器风格，即
春秋晚期秦国玉器的特征，不但线条转折近直角
形，而且雕刻草率，这或许是秦国制玉工艺落后
的表现。这件玉璜有可能是从秦国传来的。

The corners of the geometric cloud pattern are almost right
angles, this is the characteristics of the Qin-style jades, or the
jades of the Qin State in the late Spring-and-Autumn Period. This
jade *huang*-semicircular pendant might be imported from the Qin
State.

57 双龙首谷纹玉璜

Jade *Huang*-semicircular Pendant with Double-head-dragon and Grain Pattern

战国早期礼仪用玉
湖北省荆州市熊家冢墓地出土
长19、宽2.1、厚0.8厘米

Early Warring States Period
Excavated from Xiongjiazhong Cemetery of
Chu State in Jingzhou, Hubei Province
L. 19 cm, W. 2.1 cm, Th. 0.8 cm

玉质青绿色，半透明，夹黑斑，有红褐色沁。扁
平体，扇形。外缘有凸起的轮廓线，两侧雕刻
出龙首形，两龙连体。龙张口，椭圆眼，独角，
吻部凸出，龙嘴阴刻一周斜线纹，龙角阴刻网格
纹。龙身浅浮雕谷纹。中间有一圆孔。两面纹饰
相同。

58 **双龙首谷纹玉璜**
Jade *Huang*-semicircular Pendant with Double-head-dragon Pattern

战国中期礼仪用玉
湖北省荆州市江陵凤凰山墓地出土
长10、宽1.5、厚0.6厘米

Middle Warring States Period
Excavated from Fenghuangshan Cemetery of
Chu State in Jiangling, Jingzhou, Hubei Province
L. 10 cm, W. 1.5 cm, Th. 0.6 cm

玉质白色，微透明，有黑褐色沁。扁平体，扇
形。外缘有阴刻的轮廓线。两侧雕刻龙头形，两
龙连体。龙张口，椭圆形眼，独角，吻部凸出，
龙身浅浮雕谷纹。顶端有一圆穿孔。

59 双龙首勾连云纹玉璜

Jade *Huang*-semicircular Pendant with Double-
head-dragon Pattern

战国中期礼仪用玉
湖北省荆州市江陵凤凰山墓地出土
长10.1、宽0.9、厚1厘米

Middle Warring States Period
Excavated from Fenghuangshan Cemetery of
Chu State in Jiangling, Jingzhou, Hubei Province
L. 10.1 cm, W. 0.9 cm, Th. 1 cm

玉质黄白色，微透明，有黑褐色沁。扁平窄体，
扇形。外缘有阴刻的轮廓线，两侧雕刻龙头形，
两龙连体。龙头浅浮雕卷云纹，椭圆眼，吻部有
一周绹索纹，龙身碾琢勾连云纹。顶端有一竖向
圆穿孔，顶端左右两侧各有四组勾连云纹。

60 双龙首玉璜

Jade *Huang*-semicircular Pendant with Dragon Heads

战国早期礼仪用玉
湖北省荆州市熊家冢墓地出土
长5、宽1.1、厚0.4厘米

Early Warring States Period
Excavated from Xiongjiazhong Cemetery of
Chu State in Jingzhou, Hubei Province
L. 5 cm, W. 1.1 cm, Th. 0.4 cm

玉质青白色，不透明，受沁严重变成灰白色。扁
平体，扇形。两侧雕刻出对称的龙首轮廓，嘴部
呈圆孔状。顶端有一圆穿孔。

61 玉璜
Jade *Huang*-semicircular Pendant

战国早期礼仪用玉
湖北省荆州市熊家冢墓地出土
长11.3、宽2、厚0.4厘米

Early Warring States Period
Excavated from Xiongjiazhong Cemetery
of Chu State in Jingzhou, Hubei Province
L. 11.3 cm, W. 2 cm, Th. 0.4 cm

玉质黄绿色，半透明，有少量的灰色沁。扁平
体，扇形，边缘有对称的扉棱，顶部有一单面钻
圆孔。有裂痕。

62 **玉璜**
Jade *Huang*-semicircular Pendant

战国早期礼仪用玉
湖北省荆州市熊家冢墓地出土
长21.6、宽5.2、厚0.7厘米

Early Warring States Period
Excavated from Xiongjiazhong Cemetery
of Chu State in Jingzhou, Hubei Province
L. 21.6 cm, W. 5.2 cm, Th. 0.7 cm

玉质黄绿色，不透明，受沁严重变成灰黑色。扁
平体，扇形，两侧雕刻出对称的扉棱。边缘有阴
刻的打稿线，有切割痕。顶端有一单面钻圆孔。

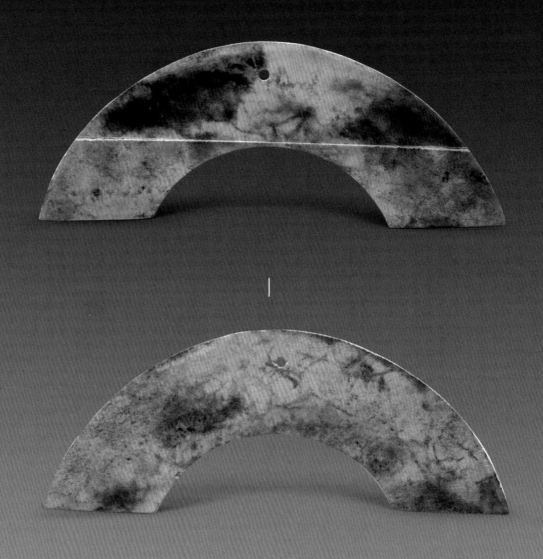

63 玉璜
Jade *Huang*-semicircular Pendant

战国早期礼仪用玉
湖北省荆州市熊家冢墓地出土
长14.9、宽3.2、厚0.4厘米

Early Warring States Period
Excavated from Xiongjiazhong Cemetery
of Chu State in Jingzhou, Hubei Province
L. 14.9 cm, W. 3.2 cm, Th. 0.4 cm

玉质青绿色，不透明，受沁严重变成灰黑色。扁平
体，扇形，素面，有切割痕。顶端有一圆穿孔。

64 **玉璜**
Jade *Huang*-semicircular Pendant

战国早期礼仪用玉
湖北省荆州市熊家冢墓地出土
长12.2、宽3、厚0.5厘米

Early Warring States Period
Excavated from Xiongjiazhong Cemetery of
Chu State in Jingzhou, Hubei Province
L. 12.2 cm, W. 3 cm, Th. 0.5 cm

玉质青绿色，不透明，受沁变成灰白色。扁平体，
扇形，两端稍宽，中部略窄。上面有一圆孔。

65 玉璜
Jade *Huang*-semicircular Pendant

战国早期礼仪用玉
湖北省荆州市熊家冢墓地出土
长12.8、宽2.7、厚0.6厘米

Early Warring States Period
Excavated from Xiongjiazhong Cemetery of
Chu State in Jingzhou, Hubei Province
L. 12.8 cm, W. 2.7 cm, Th. 0.6 cm

玉质青绿色，不透明，受沁变成灰黑色，有灰色
和褐色沁。扁平体，扇形，两端稍宽，中部略
窄。上面有一圆孔。

66 玉璜
Jade Huang-semicircular Pendant

战国时期礼仪用玉
湖北省荆州市枣林岗墓地出土
长14、宽3、厚0.5厘米

Warring States Period
Excavated from Zaolingang Cemetery
of Chu State in Jingzhou, Hubei Province
L. 14 cm, W. 3 cm, Th. 0.5 cm

玉质黄绿色，微透明，有灰黄色沁。扁平体，扇
形，素面。顶端有一圆穿孔。

67 玉璜
Jade *Huang*-semicircular Pendant

战国时期礼仪用玉
湖北省荆州市枣林岗墓地出土
长13.3、宽2.9、厚0.5厘米

Warring States Period
Excavated from Zaolingang Cemetery
of Chu State in Jingzhou, Hubei Province
L. 13.3 cm, W. 2.9 cm, Th. 0.5 cm

玉质黄绿色，微透明，有灰黄色沁。扁平体，扇
形，素面。顶端有一圆穿孔。

68 玉璜
A Pair of Jade *Huang*-semicircular Pendants

战国时期礼仪用玉
湖北省荆州市鸡公山墓地出土
上：长7.6、宽1.5、厚0.4厘米
下：长7.5、宽1.7、厚0.4厘米

Warring States Period
Excavated from Jigongshan Cemetery of
Chu State in Jingzhou, Hubei Province
Above: L. 7.6 cm, W. 1.5 cm, Th. 0.4 cm
Below: L. 7.5 cm, W. 1.7 cm, Th. 0.4 cm

一对，玉质灰黄色，不透明。扁平体，扇形，素
面。顶端有一圆穿孔。上面一件边缘有切割痕迹。

69 玉璜
Jade *Huang*-semicircular Pendant

战国时期礼仪用玉
湖北省荆州市鸡公山墓地出土
长6.8、宽1.6、厚0.4厘米

Warring States Period
Excavated from Jigongshan Cemetery of
Chu State in Jingzhou, Hubei Province
L. 6.8 cm, W. 1.6 cm, Th. 0.4 cm

玉质灰白色，不透明。扁平体，扇形，素面。顶
端有一圆穿孔。

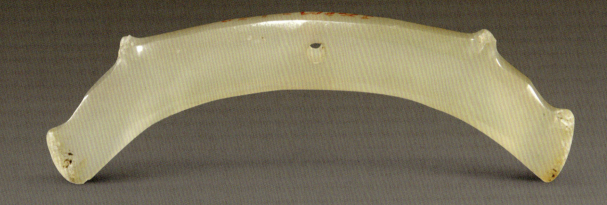

70 龙首形玛瑙璜
Chalcedony *Huang*-semicircular Pendant with
Dragon Heads Pattern

战国早期礼仪用玉
湖北省荆州市熊家冢墓地出土
长7.7、宽1、厚1厘米

Early Warring States Period
Excavated from Xiongjiazhong Cemetery of
Chu State in Jingzhou, Hubei Province
L. 7.7 cm, W. 1 cm, Th. 1 cm

玛瑙质，乳白色，半透明，有白斑。利用玛瑙料自
然形态琢磨而成。呈半圆弧形。龙首仅具轮廓，吻
部和角凸出，尾部较小。顶端有一圆穿孔。

虽然中国人制作和使用玛瑙有五千多年的历史，
但直到战国和汉代，玛瑙器仍然是制作珠、管及
小型佩饰，无容器，也没有纹饰。这是因为玛瑙
虽然坚硬，硬度甚至高过和田玉，但缺乏韧性，
它的抗压程度仅为和田玉的四十分之一，古人用
原始工具无法进行深入的加工，只能制作一些简
单的玛瑙佩饰。

Down to the Warring States Period and the Han Dynasty, the
agate in China could still be made into beads, tubes or other
small-sized ornaments. They did not bear any decorative patterns,
and no large-sized agate vessels of this time have been found.
This is because the agate is hard but not flexible and the primitive
tools could not precisely and finely enough, with which the
ancient craftsmen could only make simple and small ornaments.

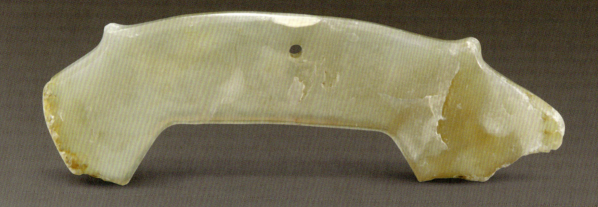

71 龙首形玛瑙璜

Chalcedony *Huang*-semicircular Pendant with Dragon Heads Pattern

战国早期礼仪用玉
湖北省荆州市熊家冢墓地出土
长8.5、宽1.7、厚0.6厘

Early Warring States Period
Excavated from Xiongjiazhong Cemetery of
Chu State in Jingzhou, Hubei Province
L. 8.5 cm, W. 1.7 cm, Th. 0.6 cm

玛瑙质，乳白色，有白斑，半透明。璜呈半圆弧
形，其两端利用玛瑙料自然形态琢磨出龙首轮
廓。吻部与鬃凸出，背部有一圆穿孔。

72 龙形玉珮
A Pair of Jade Dragon-shaped Pendants

战国早期玉佩饰
湖北省荆州市熊家冢墓地出土
上：长26.7、宽2.2~6.5、厚0.6厘米
下：长24.6、宽2.3~6.5、厚0.5厘米

Early Warring States Period
Excavated from Xiongjiazhong Cemetery of
Chu State in Jingzhou, Hubei Province
Above: L. 26.7 cm, W. 2.2~6.5 cm, Th. 0.6 cm
Below: L. 24.6 cm, W. 2.3~6.5 cm, Th. 0.5 cm

一对，玉质青白色，微透明。夹黑色点状斑，有
红褐色及黑色沁。扁平体，雕成龙形。内外缘有
阴刻轮廓线，龙回首，橄榄形眼，独角，长吻，
躬身，身下有足，长卷尾。龙吻部阴刻绚索纹。龙
身周围用细线阴刻轮廓，轮廓内浅浮雕勾连云纹。
龙角、足、尾等阴刻斜线纹。背部有一圆穿孔。

73 龙形玉珮
Jade Dragon-shaped Pendants (2 pieces)

战国早期玉佩饰
湖北省荆州市熊家冢墓地出土
均长16.5、宽2.1~4.2、厚0.4厘米

Early Warring States Period
Excavated from Xiongjiazhong Cemetery of
Chu State in Jingzhou, Hubei Province
L. 16.5 cm, W. 2.1~4.2 cm, Th. 0.4 cm（both）

2件，玉质青白色，微透明。夹黑色条状及点状
斑，有黄色沁。扁平体，雕成龙形。龙回首，独
角，长吻，躬身，身下有足，卷尾。背部有一穿
孔。龙身有裂痕和切割痕。局部有残损。

这件龙形玉珮体现了熊家冢墓地以及同时期的一
些楚墓出土玉器的玉料特点。首先是玉料呈青白
或青黄色，比如随州曾侯乙墓玉器也是这样的，
这或许是战国早期楚国玉料的特征。其次是玉料
有黑色条状或点状斑。出土于熊家冢殉葬墓的很
多玉器质料不纯，致密度低，色泽混杂，从佩戴
角度来看，这些杂质会影响审美视觉，这说明它
们的佩戴者地位不高，也有可能是专为殉葬者制
作的，而非生前佩戴用玉。

This dragon-shaped pendant showed the features of the materials of the jades unearthed from the Chu tombs. First, the hue of the jade material is bluish-white or bluish-yellow; second, it has mottles in bar or dot shapes. Seen as ornaments, these mottles spoiled the aesthetic feelings, hinting that their owners did not have high statuses, or might just have been human victims, and these ornaments were not used by high-ranking aristocrats when they were alive.

74 龙形玉珮

Jade Dragon-shaped Pendant

战国早期玉佩饰
湖北省荆州市熊家冢墓地出土
长19.1、宽2~5、厚0.3厘米

Early Warring States Period
Excavated from Xiongjiazhong Cemetery of
Chu State in Jingzhou, Hubei Province
L. 19.1 cm, W. 2~5 cm, Th. 0.3 cm

玉质黄白色，微透明。有黑色条状及点状斑，有
红褐色沁。扁平体，雕成龙形，龙回首，独角，
长吻，躬身，身下有足，卷尾。躯体下面的附饰
以及尾尖似为凤鸟。两面纹饰相同。背部有一穿
孔。龙身有裂痕和切割痕，局部有残损。

75 龙形玉珮
A Pair of Jade Dragon-shaped Pendants

战国早期玉佩饰
湖北省荆州市熊家冢墓地出土
左：长17.5、宽2.5~6.4、厚0.5厘米
右：长18.3、宽2.8~6.9、厚0.5厘米

Early Warring States Period
Excavated from Xiongjiazhong Cemetery of
Chu State in Jingzhou, Hubei Province
Left: L. 17.5 cm, W. 2.5~6.4 cm, Th. 0.5 cm
Right: L. 18.3 cm, W. 2.8~6.9 cm, Th. 0.5 cm

一对，玉质青绿色，微透明。夹黑色点状斑，有
黄色沁。扁平体，雕成龙形，龙回首，橄榄形
眼，独角，勾喙，躬身，身下有足，卷尾。吻部
和腹部连在一起。腹部有一穿孔。龙身周围用细
线阴刻轮廓，轮廓内浅浮雕勾连谷纹。吻、角、
足、尾等部位阴刻斜线纹。有切割痕。

76 **龙形玉珮**
A Pair of Jade Dragon-shaped Pendants

战国早期玉佩饰
湖北省荆州市熊家冢墓地出土
左：长10、宽6.5、厚0.7厘米
右：长10、宽7、厚0.7厘米

Early Warring States Period
Excavated from Xiongjiazhong Cemetery of
Chu State in Jingzhou, Hubei Province
Left: L. 10 cm, W. 6.5 cm, Th. 0.7 cm
Right: L. 10 cm, W. 7 cm, Th. 0.7 cm

一对，玉质黄绿色，半透明。夹黑色斑，有红褐
色沁。扁平体，雕成龙形。龙低首，椭圆眼，
躬身，身下有足，卷尾。腹部有一穿孔。龙身周
围用细线阴刻轮廓，轮廓内浅浮雕卷云纹及网格
纹。角、足、尾等阴刻斜线纹。龙身微残。

77 龙形玉珮
A Pair of Jade Dragon-shaped Pendants

战国早期玉佩饰
湖北省荆州市熊家冢墓地出土
上：长11.4、宽1.6~5.4、厚0.5厘米
下：长11.2、宽1.6~5.4、厚0.4厘米

Early Warring States Period
Excavated from Xiongjiazhong Cemetery of
Chu State in Jingzhou, Hubei Province
Above: L. 11.4 cm, W. 1.6−5.4 cm, Th. 0.5 cm
Below: L. 11.2 cm, W. 1.6−5.4 cm, Th. 0.4 cm

一对，玉质黄白色，微透明。有红褐色及灰白色
沁。扁平体，雕成龙形，龙回首，椭圆眼，独
角，躬身，身下有足，卷尾。躯体下面的附饰以
及尾尖似为凤鸟。龙身周围用细线阴刻轮廓，轮
廓内浅浮雕勾连云纹。吻、角、足、尾等部位阴
刻斜线纹。腹中有一圆穿孔。

78 龙形玉珮
Jade Dragon-shaped Pendant

战国早期玉佩饰
湖北省荆州市熊家冢墓地出土
长10.3、宽4.2、厚0.5厘米

Early Warring States Period
Excavated from Xiongjiazhong Cemetery of
Chu State in Jingzhou, Hubei Province
L. 10.3 cm, W. 4.2 cm, Th. 0.5 cm

玉质青白色，微透明，有灰白色沁。扁平体，雕
成龙形，龙回首，圆眼，拱身，卷尾。内外缘
有凸起的轮廓线，中间浅浮雕谷纹。足、尾阴刻
斜线纹。两面纹饰相同。器身共有五个圆孔。龙
身、尾有部分残损。

79 龙形玉珮

Jade Dragon-shaped Pendants

战国早期玉佩饰
湖北省荆州市熊家冢墓地出土
长9.9、宽7.8、厚0.5厘米

Early Warring States Period
Excavated from Xiongjiazhong Cemetery of
Chu State in Jingzhou, Hubei Province
L. 9.9 cm, W. 7.8 cm, Th. 0.5 cm

玉质青绿色，微透明，有灰白色及黄褐色沁。扁
平体，雕成龙形，龙回首，拱身，卷尾。身下
连接一个似凤鸟状的装饰。内外缘有阴刻的轮廓
线，中间阴刻勾连云纹。角、足、尾阴刻斜线
纹。两面纹饰相同。身上有一圆孔。

80 龙形玉珮
Jade Dragon-shaped Pendants

战国早期玉佩饰
湖北省荆州市熊家冢墓地出土
长13.9、宽2~5.3、厚0.5厘米

Early Warring States Period
Excavated from Xiongjiazhong Cemetery of Chu State in
Jingzhou, Hubei Province
L. 13.9 cm, W. 2~5.3 cm, Th. 0.5 cm

玉质黄绿色，微透明，表面有灰白色沁。扁平
体，龙回首，张口，独角，拱身，卷尾。内外缘
有阴刻的轮廓线，中间阴刻勾连云纹。角、足、
尾阴刻斜线纹。腹中部有一穿孔。

点 评
Commentary

从这件龙形玉珮上可以看出沁色有两种，即表面
的灰白色沁和下面的褐色沁，也可以理解为前者
是较重的沁，而后者是较轻的沁。凡呈灰白色沁
者（或曰鸡骨白），其玉质物理结构（如密度和
硬度）已发生改变；而褐色沁者，只是玉色有变
化（或为铁元素所致），物理结构并未改变。

This dragon-shaped jade pendant has two kinds of erosion
colors, which are the grayish-white erosion color on the surface
and the brown erosion color in the texture. The former is also
called "chicken bone white", the physical natures (density and
hardness) have been changed; the latter is only the change of the
color (caused by the iron element in the texture) but the physical
natures are not changed.

81 龙形玉珮
A Pair of Jade Dragon-shaped Pendants

战国早期玉珮饰
湖北省荆州市熊家冢墓地出土
左：长15、宽2.5、厚0.6厘米
右：长14.1、宽2.2、厚0.6厘米

Early Warring States Period
Excavated from Xiongjiazhong Cemetery of
Chu State in Jingzhou, Hubei Province
Left: L. 15 cm, W. 2.5 cm, Th. 0.6 cm
Right: L. 14.1 cm, W. 2.2 cm, Th. 0.6 cm

一对，玉质黄绿色，有黑褐色及灰白色沁，微透
明。龙回首，拱身，卷尾，腹中有一圆穿孔。龙
身的内外缘有凸起的轮廓线，中间浅浮雕谷纹，
龙角、足、尾阴刻斜线纹。上面的龙足有残损。

点 评
Commentary

有很多战国时期造型复杂的龙形玉珮上，多少可以看出一些凤鸟纹饰的元素，只是不太明显。比如上面那件玉龙的向下翻卷的尾尖，很像凤鸟的钩喙，而下面那件玉龙腹部下附饰的端部也很像一个凤鸟的头部。

On many dragon-shaped jade pendants of the Warring States Period with complicated shapes, more or less elements of phoenix or bird motifs can be seen, such as the downward curling tail of the jade dragon on the top, which looks like the hooked bill of a phoenix and the part below the belly of the jade dragon at the bottom looks like the head of a phoenix or bird.

82 **龙形玉珮**
A Pair of Jade Dragon-shaped Pendants

战国早期玉佩饰
湖北省荆州市熊家冢墓地出土
左：残长10.1、厚0.4厘米
右：残长9.5、厚0.4厘米

Early Warring States Period
Excavated from Xiongjiazhong Cemetery of
Chu State in Jingzhou, Hubei Province
Left: Remain L. 10.1 cm, Th. 0.4 cm
Right: Remain L. 9.5 cm, Th. 0.4 cm

一对，玉质青绿色，半透明，夹黑斑及褐色沁。
扁平体，龙形，龙回首，圆眼，张口，拱身，卷
尾。内外缘有阴刻轮廓线，中间碾琢谷纹，龙身
有一圆孔，背面有切割痕。上面的龙首、足、尾
都有残断，下面的龙足、尾残断。

点 评
Commentary

这两件玉龙虽然残断，但仍可看出是由一件玉龙横向一分为二而成，属于"成型对开"的制作方法。"成型对开"法的好处在于省工省料，而且两件玉器尺寸和重量基本一致，便于组珮中对称和平衡。这件玉龙的穿孔附近有斜向切割痕迹，应该是"成型对开"时开始入刀解玉时留下的。

These two jade dragons are made by splitting one jade dragon in two transversely, which is a technique called "halving a done shape". Its advantages are the labors and materials could both be saved and the two products are almost identical in size and weight, and could be symmetrically and balanced arranged in the set ornament.

83 龙形玉珮
Jade Dragon-shaped Pendant

战国中期玉佩饰
湖北省荆州市院墙湾墓地出土
长3.7、宽1.5、厚0.6厘米

Middle Warring States Period
Excavated from Yuanqiangwan Cemetery of
Chu State in Jingzhou, Hubei Province
L. 3.7 cm, W. 1.5 cm, Th. 0.6 cm

玉质乳白色，半透明，有褐斑。扁平体，雕成龙
形，龙圆眼，张口、吐舌，独角，拱身，身下有
足，卷尾。呈伏卧状。龙角、足部阴刻斜线纹。
两面纹饰相同。

点 评
Commentary

到战国中期时，楚国的玉料发生了变化，开始出
现温润细腻的和田白玉籽料作品，比如像这件龙
形玉珮和枣阳九连墩楚墓出土的白玉佩饰。但这
些白玉佩饰的尺寸比其他青黄色玉和碧玉的佩饰
都小得多，说明它们应该是用小型和田籽料雕成
的。由于籽料质地坚硬，致密度高，因此可以雕
刻出非常细腻流畅的纹饰。

In the mid Warring States Period, the materials of the jades of the
Chu State changed, and the artworks made of Khotan pebble
jade with gentle and fine texture appeared. Because the Khotan
pebble jade is hard and fine and close in texture, very exquisite
and delicate designs could be engraved out of it.

84 龙形玉珮
Jade Dragon-shaped Pendant

战国中期玉佩饰
湖北省荆州市院墙湾墓地出土
长10.5、宽3.5、厚0.4厘米

Middle Warring States Period
Excavated from Yuanqiangwan Cemetery of
Chu State in Jingzhou, Hubei Province
L. 10.5 cm, W. 3.5 cm, Th. 0.4 cm

玉质青白色，半透明，有红褐色沁。扁平体，雕
成龙形，龙昂首，张口，拱身，卷尾。内外缘有
阴刻的轮廓线，中间阴刻勾连云纹。角、足、尾
阴刻斜线纹。有切割痕。部分有残损。

85 龙形玉珮
A Pair of Jade Dragon-shaped Pendants

战国中期玉佩饰
湖北省荆州市院墙湾墓地出土
左：长16.4、宽7.1、厚0.5厘米
右：长18、宽6.7、厚0.5厘米

Middle Warring States Period
Excavated from Yuanqiangwan Cemetery of
Chu State in Jingzhou, Hubei Province
Left: L. 16.4 cm, W. 7.1 cm, Th. 0.5 cm
Right: L. 18 cm, W. 6.7 cm, Th. 0.5 cm

一对，玉质青白色，半透明，有黑色、褐色沁。
扁平体，雕成龙形，龙回首，拱身，卷尾。内
外缘有阴刻的轮廓线，中间阴刻勾连云纹。角、
足、尾阴刻斜线纹。龙身中部有一圆穿孔，有切
割痕。

86 龙形玉珮
Jade Dragon-shaped Pendant

战国中期玉佩饰
湖北省荆州市院墙湾墓地出土
长8.9、宽3.6、厚0.4厘米

Middle Warring States Period
Excavated from Yuanqiangwan Cemetery of
Chu State in Jingzhou, Hubei Province
L. 8.9 cm, W. 3.6 cm, Th. 0.4 cm

玉质青绿色，微透明，有黑褐色沁。扁平体，雕
成龙形，龙回首，长吻，独角，橄榄形眼，拱
身，卷尾。内外缘有阴刻的轮廓线，中间阴刻勾
连云纹。角、足、尾阴刻斜线纹。有切割痕。部
分有残损，龙身中部有一圆穿孔。

87 龙形玉珮
A Pair of Jade Dragon-shaped Pendants

战国中期玉佩饰
湖北省荆州市院墙湾墓地出土
上：长10.9、宽1.6、厚0.4厘米
下：长11.7、宽1.7、厚0.4厘米

Middle Warring States Period
Excavated from Yuanqiangwan Cemetery of
Chu State in Jingzhou, Hubei Province
Above: L. 10.9 cm, W. 1.6 cm, Th. 0.4 cm
Below: L. 11.7 cm, W. 1.7 cm, Th. 0.4 cm

一对，玉质绿色，半透明。扁平体，雕成龙形，
龙俯首，拱身，卷尾。内外缘有阴刻的轮廓线，
中间阴刻勾连云纹。背部有一个圆穿孔。

88 龙形玉珮
A Pair of Jade Dragon-shaped Pendants

战国中期玉佩饰
湖北省荆州市院墙湾墓地出土
左：长13.3、宽1.3、厚0.5厘米
右：长14、宽1.3、厚0.6厘米

Middle Warring States Period
Excavated from Yuanqiangwan Cemetery of
Chu State in Jingzhou, Hubei Province
Left: L. 13.3 cm, W. 1.3 cm, Th. 0.5 cm
Right: L. 14 cm, W. 1.3 cm, Th. 0.6 cm

一对，玉质青白色，微透明，有黑褐色沁。扁平
体，雕成龙形，龙回首，圆眼，张口，长吻，长
角，拱身，卷尾。内外缘有凸起的轮廓线，中间
碾琢谷纹。

89 **龙形玉珮**
Jade Dragon-shaped Pendant

战国中期玉佩饰
湖北省荆州市江陵凤凰山墓地出土
长8.2、宽3.9、厚0.5厘米

Middle Warring States Period
Excavated from Fenghuangshan Cemetery of
Chu State in Jiangling, Jingzhou, Hubei Province
L. 8.2 cm W. 3.9 cm, Th. 0.5 cm

玉质青白色，半透明，有黑褐色沁。扁平体，雕
成龙形，龙回首，椭圆眼，张口，拱身，卷尾。
内外缘有凸起的轮廓线，中间碾琢谷纹。角、
足、尾阴刻斜线纹。

点 评
Commentary

黑色沁常见于南方古墓出土的玉器上，尤以楚墓
为多。玉器的玉质一般较好，玉器收藏界称之为
"水坑沁"，可能与埋藏环境潮湿有关，具体形
成机理尚不清楚。

Dark erosion color is mostly seen on the jades unearthed from
the ancient tombs in southern China, especially the tombs of the
Chu State. The quality of the materials of these jades are usually
rather good and the antique jade collectors call the dark erosion
color as "water pit erosion", which might have been caused by the
burying environment.

90 龙形玉珮
Jade Dragon-shaped Pendant

战国中期玉佩饰
湖北省荆州市江陵凤凰山墓地出土
长13、宽1、厚0.8厘米

Middle Warring States Period
Excavated from Fenghuangshan Cemetery of
Chu State in Jiangling, Jingzhou, Hubei Province
L. 13 cm, W. 1 cm, Th. 0.8 cm

玉质青白色，表面有黑色沁。圆雕成龙形，龙张
口，椭圆眼，长吻，独角，拱身，扬尾。龙身细
长，浅浮雕细密的绞丝纹，背上有一长方形钮，
钮上有一圆穿孔。

91 龙形玉珮
Jade Dragon-shaped Pendant

战国中期玉佩饰
湖北省荆州市范家坡墓地出土
长12.7、宽7、厚0.4厘米

Middle Warring States Period
Excavated from Fanjiapo Cemetery of
Chu State in Jingzhou, Hubei Province
L. 12.7 cm, W. 7 cm, Th. 0.4 cm

玉质青绿色，半透明，夹黑斑，有橘黄色沁。扁
平体，雕成龙形。龙回首，拱身，卷尾。龙身
内外缘阴刻轮廓线，中间阴刻谷纹。龙眼用阴刻
卷云纹表现，角、足、尾阴刻线纹。两面纹饰相
同。嘴上及龙身中部有一圆孔。

92 龙形玉珮

Jade Dragon-shaped Pendant

战国中期玉佩饰
湖北省荆州市范家坡墓地出土
长9.3、宽7.9、厚0.4厘米

Middle Warring States Period
Excavated from Fanjiapo Cemetery of
 Chu State in Jingzhou, Hubei Province
L. 9.3 cm, W. 7.9 cm, Th. 0.4 cm

玉质青白色，微透明，表面有灰黄色沁。扁平
体，雕成龙形，龙回首，卷角，拱身，卷尾。龙
身内外缘阴刻轮廓线，中间碾琢谷纹。角、足、
尾阴刻线纹。两面纹饰相同。龙眼用阴刻的卷云
纹表示，嘴上、龙身中部及足各有一圆孔。龙
身、足、尾多处残断。

93 龙形玉珮
A Pair of Jade Dragon-shaped Pendants

战国中期玉佩饰
湖北省荆州市范家坡墓地出土
上：长8.1、宽1.2、厚0.4厘米
下：长8.2、宽1.2、厚0.4厘米

Middle Warring States Period
Excavated from Fanjiapo Cemetery of
Chu State in Jingzhou, Hubei Province
Above: L. 8.1 cm, W. 1.2 cm, Th. 0.4 cm
Below: L. 8.2 cm, W. 1.2 cm, Th. 0.4 cm

一对，玉质青白色，半透明，局部有灰褐色沁。
扁平体，雕成龙形，龙俯首，张口，拱身，身下
有足，卷尾。内外缘有阴刻的轮廓线，中间阴刻
勾连云纹。上面一件足残断。

94 **龙形玉珮**
Jade Dragon-shaped Pendant

战国中期玉佩饰
湖北省荆州市范家坡墓地出土
长16.8、宽1.9、厚0.5厘米

Middle Warring States Period
Excavated from Fanjiapo Cemetery of
Chu State in Jingzhou, Hubei Province
L. 16.8 cm, W. 1.9 cm, Th. 0.5 cm

玉质青绿色。半透明，夹黑色点状斑。扁平体，雕成龙形，龙张口，圆眼，拱身，卷尾。内外缘有阴刻的轮廓线，表面碾琢谷纹。两面纹饰相同。吻部有一周绚索纹。中部有一穿孔。龙身有裂痕。

95 龙形玉珮
A Pair of Jade Dragon-shaped Pendants

战国中期玉佩饰
湖北省荆州市范家坡墓地出土
上：长10.2、宽8.5、厚0.5厘米
下：长10.1、宽8.6、厚0.5厘米

Middle Warring States Period
Excavated from Fanjiapo Cemetery of Chu State in
Jingzhou, Hubei Province
Above: L. 10.2 cm, W. 8.5 cm, Th. 0.5 cm
Below: L. 10.1 cm, W. 8.6 cm, Th. 0.5 cm

一对，玉质深绿色，半透明。扁平体，雕成龙
形，龙俯首，拱身，卷尾。内外缘有阴刻的轮廓
线，中间碾琢谷纹。角、足、尾阴刻斜线纹。两
面纹饰相同。嘴、身及足各透雕一圆孔。

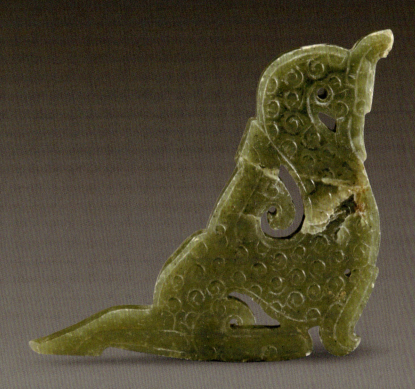

96 龙形玉珮
Jade Dragon-shaped Pendant

战国中期玉佩饰
湖北省荆州市范家坡墓地出土
长7.8、宽7.6、厚0.5厘米

Middle Warring States Period
Excavated from Fanjiapo Cemetery of
Chu State in Jingzhou, Hubei Province
L. 7.8 cm, W. 7.6 cm, Th. 0.5 cm

玉质深绿色。半透明，扁平体，雕成龙形，龙回
首，拱身，卷尾。内外缘有阴刻的轮廓线，中间
浅浮雕谷纹。角、足、尾有阴刻的线纹。两面纹饰
相同。器身有断裂痕。嘴上及身上各有一圆穿孔。

97 龙形玉珮
A Pair of Jade Dragon-shaped Pendants

战国中期玉佩饰
湖北省荆州市范家坡墓地出土
上：长15.6、宽6.1、厚0.5厘米
下：长16.5、宽6.6、厚0.6厘米

Middle Warring States Period
Excavated from Fanjiapo Cemetery of
Chu State in Jingzhou, Hubei Province
Above: L. 15.6 cm, W. 6.1 cm, Th. 0.5 cm
Below: L. 16.5 cm, W. 6.6 cm, Th. 0.6 cm

一对，玉质深绿色，微透明，表面有朱砂。扁平
体，雕成龙形，龙回首，长吻，独角，拱身，卷
尾。内外缘阴刻轮廓线，中间碾琢谷纹，龙角、
足、尾阴刻线纹。嘴上有一透雕圆孔，身上中部
也有一圆孔。器身有部分残断。

98 龙形玉珮
Jade Dragon-shaped Pendant

战国中期玉佩饰
湖北省荆州市范家坡墓地出土
长11.6、宽4.8、厚0.5厘米

Middle Warring States Period
Excavated from Fanjiapo Cemetery of Chu State in
Jingzhou, Hubei Province
L. 11.6 cm, W. 4.8 cm, Th. 0.5 cm

玉质青绿色，半透明，有红褐色沁。扁平体，雕
成龙形，龙俯首，张口，长角，长吻，拱身，卷
尾。龙身上有阴刻的打稿线。中间阴刻卷云纹。
两面纹饰相同。龙口部、尾部等共有四个圆孔。

点 评
Commentary

玉器上"人"字形弧状边缘，乃是切割两件玉璧
或玉璜等弧形玉器后留下的痕迹，说明这是一件
用余料改制的玉器。另外，此器下面边缘有整齐
均匀的红褐色沁，而其他部位则没有沁色，说明
带有沁色的这部分很有可能是原来玉料的原皮，
沁色由外向里的渐变色也说明了这一点。

The arc-shaped edges on this jade are the remnants of cutting
two jade *bi*-discs, *huang*-semicircular pendants or other jades
with arc-shaped outlines, showing that it is an ornament made of
the waste of other jades.

99 龙形玉珮
Jade Dragon-shaped Pendant

战国中期玉佩饰
湖北省荆州市范家坡墓地出土
长8.9、宽8.4、厚0.5厘米

Middle Warring States Period
Excavated from Fanjiapo Cemetery of
Chu State in Jingzhou, Hubei Province
L. 8.9 cm, W. 8.4 cm, Th. 0.5 cm

玉质深绿色，半透明。表面残留有漆皮。扁平
体，雕成龙形，龙回首，长吻，独角，拱身，卷
尾。内外缘有阴刻的轮廓线，中间碾琢谷纹。两
面纹饰相同。嘴上及龙身中部透雕一圆孔。角及
足有断裂。

100 龙形玉珮
Jade Dragon-shaped Pendant

战国中期玉佩饰
湖北省荆州市江陵雨台山墓地出土
长11.9、宽11.5、厚0.7厘米

Middle Warring States Period
Excavated from Yutaishan Cemetery of
Chu State in Jiangling, Jingzhou, Hubei Province
L. 11.9 cm, W. 11.5 cm, Th. 0.7 cm

玉质深绿色，微透明，表面有朱砂。扁平体，雕
成龙形，龙回首，长吻，独角，拱身，卷尾。
内外缘有阴刻的轮廓线，中间浅浮雕谷纹。角、
足、尾有阴刻的斜线纹。两面纹饰相同。嘴上及
身上各有一圆孔。

点 评
Commentary

从商周到汉代，棺内敷施朱砂是普遍的丧葬现
象，而出土的玉器多带有朱砂痕迹。以前玉器
收藏界有"朱砂沁"一说，即指古玉器上的红
沁由朱砂所致。但从考古出土玉器来看，并非
如此。大多数出土玉器如果带有朱砂痕迹，往
往表面比较干净，沁色很少，如同这件龙形玉
珮一样，说明朱砂不但不会形成沁色，而且对
玉质有保护作用。

This dragon-shaped jade pendant bears traces of cinnabars. In
the past, there was a term "cinnabar erosion" among the jade
collectors, which suggests that the red erosion color was caused
by the cinnabars. However, the archaeologically unearthed jades
denied this suggestion. Cinnabars not only make no harm to the
jades but can protect the jade texture.

101 龙形玉珮
Jade Dragon-shaped Pendant

战国中期玉佩饰
湖北省荆州市杨场墓地出土
长17、宽7、厚0.5厘米

Middle Warring States Period
Excavated from Yangchang Cemetery of
Chu State in Jingzhou, Hubei Province
L. 17 cm, W. 7 cm, Th. 0.5 cm

玉质青绿色，微透明。有少量黄褐色沁，表面布
满了灰白色沁。扁平体，雕成龙形，龙回首，
独角，圆眼，拱身，卷尾。内外缘有阴刻的轮廓
线，中间碾琢谷纹，角、足、尾阴刻线纹。两面
纹饰相同。嘴上透雕一圆孔，身、足、尾各有一
圆孔。边缘有残损。

102 龙形玉珮
Jade Dragon-shaped Pendant

战国中期玉佩饰
湖北省荆州市杨场墓地出土
长13.5、宽6、厚0.5厘米

Middle Warring States Period
Excavated from Yangchang Cemetery of Chu State in
Jingzhou, Hubei Province
L. 13.5 cm, W. 6 cm, Th. 0.5 cm

玉质青绿色，微透明，有灰白色沁。扁平体，雕
成龙形，龙俯首，长吻，独角，圆眼，拱身，
卷尾。内外缘有阴刻的轮廓线，中间碾琢谷纹，
角、足、尾阴刻线纹。两面纹饰相同。嘴上透雕一
圆孔，身、足、尾各有一圆孔。器身上有断裂痕。

103 双龙形玉珮

Jade Pendant in the Shape of Double Dragons

战国早期玉佩饰
湖北省荆州市熊家冢墓地出土
长11.8、宽5.9、厚0.6厘米

Early Warring States Period
Excavated from Xiongjiazhong Cemetery of
Chu State in Jingzhou, Hubei Province
L. 11.8 cm, W. 5.9 cm, Th. 0.6 cm

玉质青白色，不透明，有裂痕。扁平体，长方
形，透雕成龙形，未刻画细部。两龙相背，龙回
首，拱身，卷尾。两龙的身下和中部共透雕三个
等距离分布的玉璧。

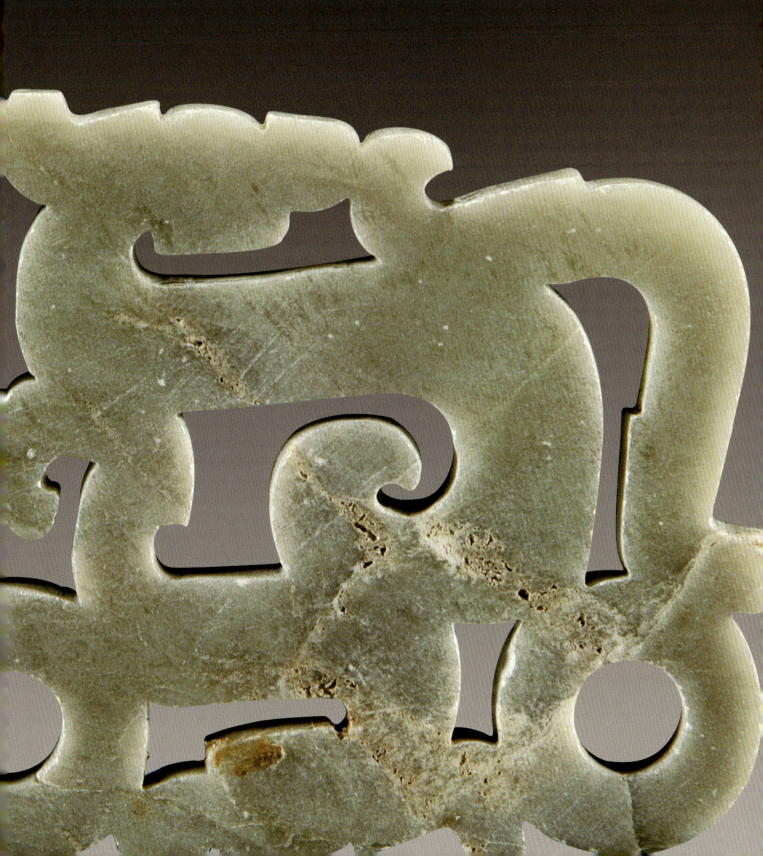

104 **双龙形玉珮**
Jade Pendant in the Shape of Double Dragons

战国早期玉佩饰
湖北省荆州市熊家冢墓地出土
长10.6、宽6.2、厚0.5厘米

Early Warring States Period
Excavated from Xiongjiazhong Cemetery of
Chu State in Jingzhou, Hubei Province
L. 10.6 cm, W. 6.2 cm, Th. 0.5 cm

玉质青白色，不透明。扁平体，长方形，透雕成
龙形，未刻画细部。两龙相背，龙回首，拱身，
卷尾。两龙的左右各攀附一条小龙，龙头朝下。
小龙的身下各透雕一小璧，大龙的中间透雕一个
大璧，三个璧等距离分布。

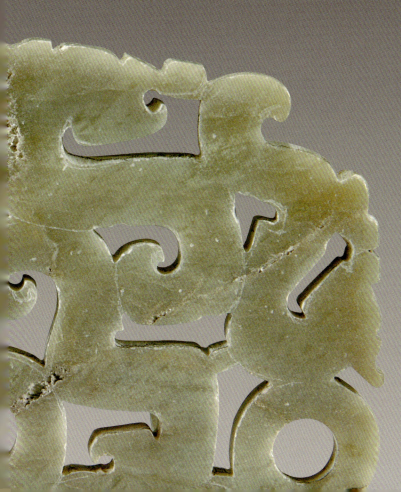

105 **双龙形玉珮**
Jade Pendant in the Shape of Double Dragons

战国中期玉佩饰
湖北省荆州市院墙湾墓地出土
长8、宽3.1、厚0.6厘米

Middle Warring States Period
Excavated from Yuanqiangwan Cemetery of Chu State in
Jingzhou, Hubei Province
L. 8 cm, W. 3.1 cm, Th. 0.6 cm

玉质乳白色，夹少许黑点，半透明，有橘黄色及
黑褐色沁。扁平体，椭圆形。内外分别雕刻两条
龙，内区的两龙连体。龙圆眼，张口，长吻向下
内勾，独角。外区的两龙吻部相连，独角，长吻
向上翻卷，身体向上卷曲，中部有一穿孔。龙身
四周有凸起的轮廓线，角、足、尾阴刻斜线纹，
内碾琢谷纹。

106 双龙形玉珮
Jade Pendant in the Shape of Double Dragons

战国中期玉佩饰
湖北省荆州市江陵雨台山墓地出土
长5.6、宽3.3、厚0.4厘米

Middle Warring States Period
Excavated from Yutaishan Cemetery of
Chu State in Jiangling, Jingzhou, Hubei Province
L. 5.6 cm, W. 3.3 cm, Th. 0.4 cm

玉质黄绿色，不透明，受沁变成灰黄色。扁平体，雕成两龙，两龙连体，龙角相连，无细部雕刻。龙回首，拱身，卷尾。龙的中间有一个方璧形饰，中间有一个圆孔。

107 双龙形玉珮
Jade Pendant in the Shape of Double Dragons

战国时期玉佩饰
湖北省荆州市鸡公山墓地出土
长5.7、宽3.3、厚0.5厘米

Warring States Period
Excavated from Jigongshan Cemetery of Chu State in
Jingzhou, Hubei Province
L. 5.7 cm, W. 3.3 cm, Th. 0.5 cm

玉质淡绿色，不透明。扁平体，透雕左右对称的龙纹，只简单地雕出龙头及龙尾，没有阴刻细部。

点 评
Commentary

这种质料不透明的玉器一般雕工较为简单，似专为丧葬之用。玉器表面有细密杂乱的划痕，说明质料较软，应为石质，是玉料的替代品，也说明使用者的身份等级较低。

This dragon-shaped jade pendant seems to be made specially for burying. The thin and random incising traces on this pendant show that the texture is soft, so it might be stone instead of jade, and its owner had low status.

108 龙凤形玉珮

Jade Pendant in the Shape of a Dragon and a Phoenix

战国早期玉佩饰
湖北省荆州市熊家冢墓地出土
长12.7、宽9.1、厚0.5厘米

Early Warring States Period
Excavated from Xiongjiazhong Cemetery of
Chu State in Jingzhou, Hubei Province
L. 12.7 cm, W. 9.1 cm, Th. 0.5 cm

玉质黄绿色，微透明，有黑色絮状斑及橘黄色
沁。扁平体，雕成龙凤形，左龙，右凤，龙凤连
体。龙回首，张口，圆眼，长角，拱身，卷尾，
呈伏卧状。腹中有一穿孔。凤钩喙，独角，俯
卧在龙尾上，与龙相比，雕刻较简练。尾部缺
失。龙身周围用细线阴刻轮廓，轮廓内浅浮雕卷
云纹，龙角、足、尾阴刻斜线纹，凤身阴刻鱼鳞
纹，尾部阴刻斜线纹。

109 龙凤形玉珮

Jade Pendant in the Shape of a Dragon and a Phoenix

战国早期玉佩饰
湖北省荆州市熊家冢墓地出土
长18.1、宽5、厚0.8厘米

Excavated from Xiongjiazhong Cemetery of
Chu State in Jingzhou, Hubei Province
L. 18.1 cm, W. 5 cm, Th. 0.8 cm

玉质黄绿色，微透明，有灰白、灰青色沁。一龙
一凤形，龙曲颈，蜷躯，卷尾，凤栖于龙尾部，
钩喙回首。龙颈下部钻一孔，其中一面的龙头颈
部和腹部各有一道切割痕。龙体边缘刻一周阴线
边廓，首部刻龙眼、鼻、角，足部刻龙爪，尾部刻斜
线纹，躯干刻云纹、谷纹。凤身刻羽纹。

110 龙凤形玉珮
Jade Pendant in the Shape of a Dragon and a
Phoenix

战国晚期玉佩饰
湖北省荆州市秦家山墓地出土
长5.4、宽1.8、厚0.5厘米

Late Warring States Period
Excavated from Qinjiashan Cemetery of
Chu State in Jingzhou, Hubei Province
L. 5.4, W. 1.8 cm, Th. 0.5 cm

玉质乳白色，微透明。透雕龙凤纹，龙凤相背，
均为圆眼，独角，卷尾，尾部以长方形珩相连，
饰网格纹。一侧残断。两面纹饰相同。

111 双首龙形玉珮
Jade Pendant in the Shape of a Double-head-dragon

战国中期玉佩饰
湖北省荆州市院墙湾墓地出土
长5.2、宽1.1、厚0.6厘米

Middle Warring States Period
Excavated from Yuanqiangwan Cemetery of
Chu State in Jingzhou, Hubei Province
L. 5.2 cm, W. 1.1 cm, Th. 0.6 cm

玉质乳白色，半透明。扁平体，雕成龙形。两龙
连体，龙首造型有异，均为独角，长吻，共有四
个穿孔。龙身碾琢谷纹。

点 评
Commentary

古玉的受沁状况，除了与埋藏环境有关外，与玉质的致密程度关系很大。玉质越好，致密度就越大，越不易受到侵蚀。此器玉质温润致密（可能是和田籽料），表面打磨抛光精细，所以虽然在地下埋藏两千多年，出土后仍光亮如新，看不出沁色的痕迹。

The erosion severities of ancient jades have close relationship with the densities of the jade textures. The better jade had the higher density and the less possibility to be eroded. The texture of this jade object is fine, gentle and dense, and the surface is ground and polished precisely and smoothly, so it looks still like new after being buried underground for more than 2000 years without any traces of erosion.

（正）

112　龙鸟蛇形玉珮

Jade Pendant in the Shape of Dragons, Birds, and Snake

战国中期玉佩饰
湖北省荆州市院墙湾墓地出土
长6.5、宽3、厚0.5厘米

Middle Warring States Period
Excavated from Yuanqiangwan Cemetery of
Chu State in Jingzhou, Hubei Province
L. 6.5, W. 3 cm, Th. 0.5 cm

玉质乳白色，夹黑色点状斑，半透明，有黑褐色
沁。扁平体，雕成龙鸟形。左右两侧各雕刻一
个昂首、拱身、卷尾的龙。两龙相背，中间有一
条盘曲成椭圆形的蛇。龙的头部分别站立一只小
鸟，小鸟的喙叼住位于龙尾的鱼。龙足蹬一条形
装饰。龙张口，圆形眼，独角。龙身四周阴刻轮
廓线，内饰鱼鳞纹。鸟独角，翘尾，鸟身阴刻鱼
鳞纹，蛇身阴刻卷云纹。龙角、尾和鸟冠、尾阴
刻斜线纹。每面有六个对称的凹坑。

（背）

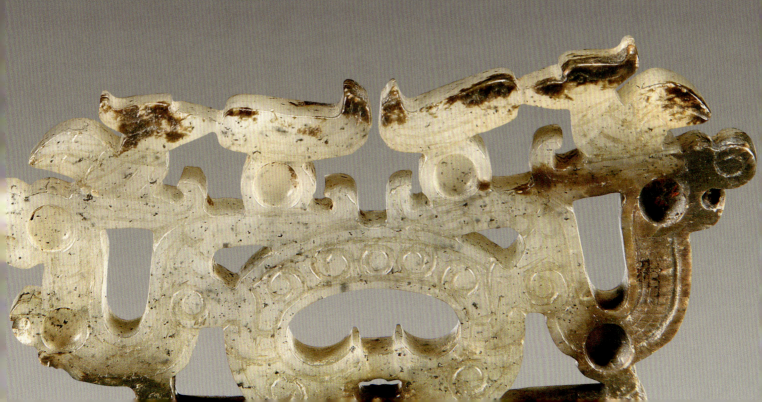

113 神人乘龙形玉珮

Jade Pendant in the Shape of a Human Deity
Riding a Dragon

战国早期玉佩饰
湖北省荆州市熊家冢墓地出土
长11.7、宽7.9、厚0.4厘米

Early Warring States Period
Excavated from Xiongjiazhong Cemetery of
Chu State in Jingzhou, Hubei Province
L. 11.7 cm, W. 7.9 cm, Th. 0.4 cm

玉质青绿色，有灰白色沁。扁平体，雕成龙形，
龙回首，拱身，卷尾，足上站立一神人。龙张
口，椭圆眼，长吻，角断裂。龙身内外缘阴刻轮
廓线，中间阴刻勾连云纹。足、尾阴刻线纹。神
人椭圆脸，弧形耳，长裙衫。阴刻眼、鼻、嘴，
双手放在胸前。阴刻网格纹服饰。左手可以看见
手指。由于切割的原因，神人右侧出现了一定的
错位。

114 神人操龙形玉珮

Jade Pendant in the Shape of a Human Deity and a Dragon

战国中期玉佩饰

湖北省荆州市院墙湾墓地出土

长7.2、宽3.4、厚0.4厘米

Middle Warring States Period
Excavated from Yuanqiangwan Cemetery of
Chu State in Jingzhou, Hubei Province
L. 7.2, W. 3.4 cm, Th. 0.4 cm

玉质黄白色，半透明，有黑褐色沁。扁平体，雕成龙形。两龙相对，龙昂首，张口，圆眼，独角，拱身，卷尾。两龙用吻部托起一璧。下面龙身中间站立一神人，神人两手抓住龙身，头部顶起璧。龙背各托起一只神鸟。龙身阴刻卷云纹、鱼鳞纹。神鸟圆眼，钩喙，翘尾站立在龙身上。神鸟身上饰鱼鳞纹。龙及神鸟的尾部都阴刻线纹。璧中间饰绹索纹。神人阴刻眼睛、鼻子、嘴巴及网格纹服饰。

点 评
Commentary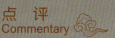

荆州楚墓中出土的神人与龙形象的玉器，是最具有地方文化特色的器物，这种纹饰还常见于漆器（包括漆棺）和纺织品。虽然目前对这类纹饰的具体含义尚不清楚，但它却是楚玉的一个特征，对于判断传世的战国时期神人与龙共体玉器的文化归属是有意义的。另外，熊家冢墓地出土的神人乘龙形玉珮（见图版113）也与此器类似，造型恰为此器的一半。

The jades in the shape of human deity and dragon joined together are the jade objects with the most local cultural features and they are one of the characteristics of the jades of the Chu State, which is meaningful for estimating the cultural attribution of the handed-down human-dragon joint-shaped jades of the Warring-States Period. In addition, the jade pendant in the shape of a human deity riding a dragon (see Plate 113) unearthed from Xiongjiazhong Cemetery has similar shape with this pendant and is exactly a half of it.

115 透雕云纹玉珮
Jade Pendant with Cloud Pattern in Openwork

战国晚期玉佩饰
湖北省荆州市秦家山墓地出土
长4.1、宽2.3、厚0.6厘米

Late Warring States Period
Excavated from Qinjiashan Cemetery of
Chu State in Jingzhou, Hubei Province
L. 4.1 cm, W. 2.3 cm, Th. 0.6 cm

玉质青白色，不透明，有橘黄色沁。外缘有扉
棱，中间阴刻谷纹，透雕钩状云纹。此系残件改
制而成。

116 三角形玉饰
Jade Pendant in the Shape of a Triangle

战国中期装饰用玉
湖北省荆州市院墙湾墓地出土
高2.5、边长2.8、厚0.4厘米

Middle Warring States Period
Excavated from Yuanqiangwan Cemetery of Chu State in
Jingzhou, Hubei Province
H. 2.5 cm, Side L. 2.8 cm, Th. 0.4 cm

玉质乳白色，半透明。扁平体，正面为等腰三角
形。中间阴刻一个带羽神鸟，下面阴刻两条神
龙。背面有一凸钮，上面有一圆孔。

117 玉觿
A Pair of Jade *Xi*-bodkin Pendants

战国中期装饰用玉
湖北省荆州市院墙湾墓地出土
上：长5.8、宽0.9、厚0.6厘米
下：长6、宽0.8、厚0.6厘米

Middle Warring States Period
Excavated from Yuanqiangwan Cemetery of Chu State in
Jingzhou, Hubei Province
Above: L. 5.8 cm, W. 0.9 cm, Th. 0.6 cm
Below: L.6 cm, W. 0.8 cm, Th. 0.6 cm

一对，玉质乳白色，不透明，上面一件受沁变
黄。角形，一端平齐，一端尖锐。平齐端有一小
穿孔。

点 评
Commentary

玉觿一般成对出土，是玉组珮最下面的佩饰，也
称玉牙。佩戴者在行动时，玉觿的摆动幅度最
大，它们可以相互撞击或与其他玉珮相击发出悦
耳的玉声，以节制步伐。

Jade *xi*-bodkins are usually unearthed in pairs; they are the lowest
parts of the jade set ornament and also called "jade teeth." When
their wearers were moving, the *xi*-bodkins waved in the largest
range and they could bump into each other or with other parts of
the set ornament to make harmonious jingles which can remind
the wearer to keep the walking speed.

118 玉琮
Jade *Cong*-Prismatic Cylinder

战国时期玉用具
湖北省荆州市紫荆砖瓦厂墓地出土
高2.1、边长5.9、孔径4.6、厚0.8厘米

Warring States Period
Excavated from Zijingzhuanwachang Cemetery of
Chu State in Jingzhou, Hubei Province
H. 2.1 cm, Side L. 5.9 cm, D.(hole) 4.6 cm, Th. 0.8 cm

玉质黄白色，微透明，有灰褐色及黄色条状纹理。
俯视呈方形体，外方内圆，无射部。光素无纹。

点 评
Commentary

此器名为玉琮，实则非标准玉琮，仅外观形似而
已。玉琮在战国时期基本绝迹，标准式样的玉琮
极少见，说明它已经退出玉礼器的行列。这件玉
器的玉料杂质多，不纯净，并非好料。从中间钻
孔痕迹来看，可能是一件半成品，也可能是作为
用具的嵌插器。

The material of this jade object is not pure enough and not good
for making artworks. From the drilling traces, we can infer that it
is a half-done product or a stand used for inserting other objects.

119 **玉琮**
Jade *Cong*-Prismatic Cylinder

战国时期玉用具
湖北省荆州市楚墓出土
高0.9、边长1.4、孔径0.6、厚0.4厘米

Warring States Period
Excavated from the Tombs of
Chu State in Jingzhou, Hubei Province
H. 0.9 cm, Side L. 1.4 cm, D.(hole) 0.6 cm, Th. 0.4 cm

玉质青白色，半透明，有黄褐色沁。长方体，中
间钻一圆孔，长方体四边角切割出射部，中间呈
八边形。

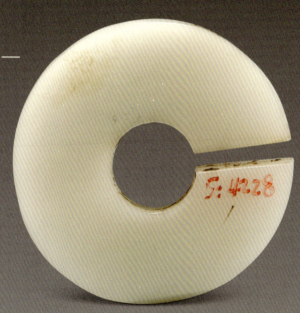

120 蟠虺纹玉玦

Jade Slit *Jue*-earring with Coiled Dragon Pattern

春秋晚期礼仪用玉
湖北省荆州市鸡公山墓地出土
直径3.4、孔径1、厚0.5厘米

Late Spring and Autumn Period
Excavated from Jigongshan Cemetery of
Chu State in Jingzhou, Hubei Province
D.(outer) 3.4 cm, D.(inner) 1 cm, Th. 0.5 cm

玉质乳白色，半透明。扁平体，圆环形，一侧有
一缺口。正面的内外缘都阴刻轮廓线，中间阴刻
四组蟠虺纹。背面光素无纹。

点 评
Commentary

玉玦为耳饰，一般成对出土。此器一面光素，应
该是将一件玉玦一剖为二，作为一对玉玦使用
的。光素的一面为切割面，还未雕上纹饰。所饰
蟠虺纹是春秋晚期的式样，而玉玦出土于战国墓
中，应为沿用的前世玉器。

Jade *jue*-earrings are always unearthed in pairs. The coiled
dragon design is the motif of the late Spring-and-Autumn
Period, but these jade *jue*-earrings are unearthed from a tomb
of the Warring States Period, so they would have been handed
down jades.

点 评
Commentary

这种式样的玉带钩传世品很多，亦有很多仿品。鉴定时要注意：1. 钩首与钩身相连的凹槽处要有一定宽度，至少可以容下钩环的厚度；2. 钩钮要有一定的高度，至少可以容下皮带的宽度。

Two features must be observed when this type of belt hooks are authenticated and identified: 1. the bending angle of the hook head and the hook body must be wide enough for the belt ring; 2. the hook button must be high enough for the thickness of the leather belt.

121 龙首玉带钩
Jade Belt Hook with Dragon Head Pattern

战国时期实用玉器
湖北省荆州市鸡公山墓地出土
长5.8、宽1、厚0.9厘米

Warring States Period
Excavated from Jigongshan Cemetery of
Chu State in Jingzhou, Hubei Province
L. 5.8 cm, W. 1 cm, Th. 0.9 cm

玉质黄白色，微透明，有褐色沁。钩首为龙首形，钩腹扁长，钩钮呈长方形。

122 龙首玉带钩
Jade Belt Hook with Dragon Head Pattern

战国时期实用玉器
湖北省荆州市楚墓出土
长5.7、宽2.6、厚0.8厘米

Warring States Period
Excavated from the Tombs of
Chu State in Jingzhou, Hubei Province
L. 5.7 cm, W. 2.6 cm, Th. 0.8 cm

玉质鸡骨白色，不透明，有黄褐色铁锈沁。钩首为龙首形，阴刻出龙的眼和嘴，钩钮呈椭圆形。

123 龙首玉带钩
Jade Belt Hook with Dragon Head Pattern

战国晚期实用玉器
湖北省荆州市天星观墓地出土
长7.5、宽1.5、厚1厘米

Late Warring States Period
Excavated from Tianxingguan Cemetery of
Chu State in Jingzhou, Hubei Province
L. 7.5 cm, W. 1.5 cm, Th. 1 cm

玉质鸡骨白色，不透明，有土沁。钩首为龙首
形，钩腹上起两道凸棱，钩钮呈长方形。

124 龙首玉带钩
Jade Belt Hook with Dragon Head Pattern

战国晚期实用玉器
湖北省荆州市谢家桥墓地出土
长6.6、宽1.7、厚1.7厘米

Late Warring States Period
Excavated from Xiejiaqiao Cemetery of
Chu State in Jingzhou, Hubei Province
L. 6.6 cm, W. 1.7 cm, Th. 1.7 cm

玉质黄褐色，不透明，有灰黑色沁。钩体俯视呈琵
琶形，钩首为龙首形，钩腹光素，钩钮呈椭圆形。

（正）

125 谷纹玉剑首
Jade Sword Pommel with Grain Pattern

战国中期玉剑饰
湖北省荆州市院墙湾墓地出土
直径4.8、孔径1.9、厚0.4厘米

Middle Warring States Period
Excavated from Yuanqiangwan Cemetery of
Chu State in Jingzhou, Hubei Province
D.(outer) 4.8 cm, D.(inner) 1.9 cm, Th. 0.4 cm

玉质青白色，半透明，夹黑色点状斑。扁平体，
圆形，由璧和圆钮组成，圆钮置于璧中孔，可以
随意取下。璧正面外缘有阴刻的轮廓线，碾琢谷
纹，背面阴刻勾连云纹。圆钮正面阴刻四朵卷云
纹，背面光素。

点 评
Commentary

此器为复合式玉剑首，较为罕见。玉剑饰是到汉代才发展成熟的，战国时期的玉剑饰出土很少，式样也不固定。这种复合式玉剑首体现出战国剑饰多样性的特点。

This is a compound jade pommel rarely seen in its counterparts. Jade sword fittings fully developed in the Han Dynasty and the jade sword fittings of the Warring States Period are not only rare but varying in styles. This compound pommel shows that the variety was the characteristics of the jade sword fittings of the Warring States Period.

（背）

126 谷纹玉剑首
Jade Sword Pommel with Grain Pattern

战国晚期玉剑饰
湖北省荆州市谢家桥墓地出土
直径4.5厘米，厚0.6厘米

Late Warring States Period
Excavated from Xiejiaqiao Cemetery of
Chu State in Jingzhou, Hubei Province
D. 4.5 cm, Th. 0.6 cm

玉质青绿色，半透明，有灰色沁。正面外缘有阴
刻的轮廓线，纹饰分为两区，外区浅浮雕谷纹，
内区浅浮雕圆涡纹。背面光素无纹，有一环槽，
以嵌剑柄。正面中间有残损。

127 谷纹玉剑首
Jade Sword Pommel with Grain Pattern

战国时期玉剑饰
湖北省荆州市岳桥印台墓地出土
直径4.5、厚1.1厘米

Warring States Period
Excavated from Yueqiaoyintai Cemetery of
Chu State in Jingzhou, Hubei Province
D. 4.5 cm, Th. 1.1 cm

玉质青绿色，微透明，有黑色沁。正面外缘有一
周阴刻的轮廓线，中间有两圈阴刻的弦纹将纹饰
分为两区，内区阴刻四朵卷云纹，中间有阴刻的
网格纹。外区饰谷纹。

（正）

128 谷纹玉剑首
Jade Sword Pommel with Grain Pattern

战国时期玉剑饰
湖北省荆州市江陵砖瓦厂墓地出土
直径7、厚2.2厘米

Warring States Period
Excavated from jianglingzhuanwachang Cemetery of
Chu State in Jingzhou, Hubei Province
D. 7 cm, Th. 2.2 cm

玉质灰白色，不透明。圆柱体，正面外缘有一周
阴刻的轮廓线，中间有两圈阴刻的弦纹将纹饰
分为两区，内区阴刻四朵卷云纹，中间有阴刻的
网格纹。外区饰谷纹。背面饰一周阴刻的勾连云
纹。边缘略残损。

点 评
Commentary

此器背面应有穿孔或环槽，以便嵌插固定剑柄，但奇怪的是此器并没有穿孔或环槽，因此，如何将剑首固定于剑柄上就有可探讨之处了，或许是用粘合的方式，或许是半成品，还未来得及做穿孔或环槽。

This jade pommel should have had perforation or groove on the reverse for fitting the sword hilt; however, it does not have perforation or groove at all. Perhaps it had been stuck to the hilt, or it was just a half-done product without the perforation or groove made.

（背）

（侧）

129 乳钉纹玉剑璏
Jade Scabbard Slide with Nipple Pattern

战国中期玉剑饰
湖北省荆州市江陵凤凰山墓地出土
长6.2、宽2.4、厚0.6~1.7厘米

Middle Warring States Period
Excavated from Fenghuangshan Cemetery of
Chu State in Jiangling, Jingzhou, Hubei Province
L. 6.2 cm, W. 2.4 cm, Th. 0.6−1.7 cm

玉质乳白色，微透明，有黑色及褐色沁。璏面正
视长方形，侧视略弧，表面阴刻网格纹及浅浮雕
乳钉纹。璏面下方有长方形穿孔。

点 评
Commentary

玉剑璏是镶嵌在剑鞘上，用以穿带固定以供佩戴
的。战国的玉剑璏比汉代的短，说明战国的剑鞘
短，可能与战国青铜剑的长度要短于汉代铁剑的
长度有关。

The jade *wei*-scabbard slide was inlayed on the scabbard
for fitting to the waist belt. The reason why the *wei* of the
Warring States Period are shorter than that of the Han Dynasty
might be that the bronze swords of the Warring States Period
are shorter than the iron swords of the Han Dynasty.

130 **龙纹玉剑璲**
Jade Scabbard Slide with Dragon Pattern

战国时期玉剑饰
湖北省荆州市岳桥印台墓地出土
高2.9、长8.6厘米

Warring States Period
Excavated from Yueqiaoyintai Cemetery of
Chu State in Jingzhou, Hubei Province
H. 2.9 cm ,L. 8.6 cm

玉质青绿色，微透明，受沁变成青黑色。璲面右
端上翘，左端下卷。两侧各有一个卷云纹装饰呈
对称分布。璲面上雕刻一条龙，龙昂首，卷尾，
单爪站立在座上。龙身阴刻卷云纹，下面有长方
形孔。

131 卷云纹玉剑珌
Jade Scabbard Chape with Cloud Pattern

战国中期玉剑饰
湖北省荆州市江陵凤凰山墓地出土
长6、宽4.7~5.7、厚1厘米

Middle Warring States Period
Excavated from Fenghuangshan Cemetery of
Chu State in Jiangling, Jingzhou, Hubei Province
L. 6 cm, W. 4.7~5.7 cm, Th. 1 cm

玉质青白色，微透明，有黑褐色沁。束腰梯形，
侧视扁圆形。四周有阴刻的轮廓线，两侧阴刻对
称的"T"形卷云纹，中间阴刻一个变形兽面纹，
圆圈表现兽眼，卷云纹代表耳朵、嘴巴等。两面
纹饰相同。顶端有一个没有穿透的圆孔，底部阴
刻一个变形兽面纹。

玉扁管是春秋战国时期常见的玉饰，属于成
套的玉组珮配件之一。玉组珮是由多件玉珮
组成，以丝线穿缀。由于玉珮之间的丝线外
露不美观，故以珠、管一类的饰品穿缀于主
要玉珮之间的丝线上，起到遮掩丝线、视之
美观的效果。

Jade set ornament is composed of many jade ornaments
linked together with silk strings. Because the exposed silk
strings gave bad visual effects, so the jade beads or tubes
are used to cover these silk strings among the main jade
ornaments to make the entire set better to see.

133 谷纹玉扁管
Jade Tubular Pendant with Grain Pattern

战国中期装饰用玉
湖北省荆州市院墙湾墓地出土
长3、宽1、厚0.8厘米

Middle Warring States Period
Excavated from Yuanqiangwan Cemetery of
Chu State in Jingzhou, Hubei Province
L. 3 cm, W. 1 cm, Th. 0.8 cm

玉质红褐色，不透明。扁平体，长条形。共四
面，每面四周有阴刻的轮廓线，中间碾琢谷纹。
通体纵向贯穿一圆孔。

132 玉戈
Jade *Ge*-dagger Ax

战国晚期礼仪玉器
湖北省荆州市天星观墓地出土
长31、宽5.3、厚1厘米

Late Warring States Period
Excavated from Tianxingguan Cemetery of
Chu State in Jingzhou, Hubei Province
L. 31 cm, W. 5.3 cm, Th. 1 cm

玉质灰褐色，不透明，有黑色沁。尖首长条形，两侧
竖直，到底端斜收成细柄，柄上有一圆形穿孔。

_134_ **谷纹玉扁管**
A Pair of Jade Tubular Pendants with Grain Pattern

战国晚期装饰用玉
湖北省荆州市天星观墓地出土
上：长5.4、宽1.7、厚0.6厘米
下：长5.4、宽1.7、厚0.8厘米

Late Warring States Period
Excavated from Tianxingguan Cemetery of
Chu State in Jingzhou, Hubei Province
Above: L. 5.4 cm, W. 1.7 cm, Th. 0.6 cm
Below: L. 5.4 cm, W. 1.7 cm, Th. 0.8 cm

一对，玉质红褐色，不透明。扁平体，长条形。
两侧有对称扉棱，两面碾琢谷纹及蝌蚪纹，一面
中间有一条凸脊。通体纵向贯穿一圆孔。

135 勾连云纹玉扁管
A Pair of Jade Tubular Pendants with Intertwined
Cloud Pattern

战国早期装饰用玉
湖北省荆州市熊家冢墓地出土
均长4.2、宽1.3、厚0.7厘米

Early Warring States Period
Excavated from Xiongjiazhong Cemetery of
Chu State in Jingzhou, Hubei Province
L. 4.2 cm, W. 1.3 cm, Th. 0.7 cm(both)

一对，玉质青绿色，不透明。扁平体，长方形，
两侧有对称的扉棱。中间阴刻勾连云纹。通体纵
向贯穿一圆孔。

136 蟠虺纹玉扁管
Jade Tubular Pendant with Coiled Dragon Pattern

战国中期装饰用玉
湖北省荆州市院墙湾墓地出土
长7.3、宽1.9、厚0.7厘米

Middle Warring States Period
Excavated from Yuanqiangwan Cemetery of
Chu State in Jingzhou, Hubei Province
L. 7.3 cm, W. 1.9 cm, Th. 0.7 cm

玉质青白色，微透明，有黑褐色沁。扁平体，长
条形。两侧雕刻对称的扉棱，中间饰阴刻的蟠虺
纹。通体纵向贯穿一圆孔。

137 蟠虺纹玉扁管
Jade Tubular Pendant with Coiled Dragon Pattern

战国时期装饰用玉
湖北省荆州市钟祥黄土坡墓地出土
长4.3、宽1.7、厚1厘米

Warring States Period
Excavated from Huangtupo Cemetery of
Chu State in Zhongxiang, Jingzhou, Hubei Province
L. 4.3 cm, W. 1.7 cm, Th. 1 cm

玉质青白色，半透明，有黄色沁。长条形，中间
阴刻蟠虺纹，两侧阴刻垂鳞纹，一角不平，经磨
光。顶部有一穿孔通至底部。一侧有残损。

一

138 兽面纹玉扁管
Jade Tubular Pendant with Animal Mask Pattern

战国早期装饰用玉
湖北省荆州市熊家冢墓地出土
长7、宽2.7、厚0.6厘米

Early Warring States Period
Excavated from Xiongjiazhong Cemetery of
Chu State in Jingzhou, Hubei Province
L. 7 cm, W. 2.7 cm, Th. 0.6 cm

玉质受沁变成青灰色，不透明。扁平体，长条
形，边缘有对称的扉棱，两面纹饰相同。内外缘
有阴刻的轮廓，中间透雕一条形穿将纹饰分为三
区。条形穿的左右两侧阴刻卷云纹，上下阴刻简
化的兽面纹、椭圆形眼、条形鼻、卷云纹耳及
嘴、网格纹眉。顶部有一圆穿孔和条形穿相通至
底部。

139 竹节形玉管

A Pair of Jade Bamboo-shaped Tubular Pendants

战国早期装饰用玉
湖北省荆州市熊家冢墓地出土
均高5.2、直径1厘米

Early Warring States Period
Excavated from Xiongjiazhong Cemetery of
Chu State in Jingzhou, Hubei Province
H. 5.2 cm, D. 1 cm (both)

一对，玉质灰绿色，不透明。圆柱形，竹节状。
中间有四道凹槽将玉管分为五节，上下节各有一
组四道较窄凸弦纹，中间有三组三道较宽的凸弦
纹。顶部有一圆穿孔通至底部。左边一件顶端残
缺一角，右边一件中间有裂痕。

140 蟠虺纹玉片
Jade Plaque with Coiled Dragon Pattern

战国时期丧葬用玉
湖北省荆州市肖家山墓地出土
长4.1、宽3.2、厚0.4厘米

Warring States Period
Excavated from Xiaojiashan Cemetery of
Chu State in Jingzhou, Hubei Province
L. 4.1 cm, W. 3.2 cm, Th. 0.4 cm

玉质黑色，不透明。扁平体，长方形，正面四周
有对称的扁棱，中间饰蟠虺纹，背面为素面。上
下两端各有两个圆穿孔。

点 评
Commentary

这种方形薄片状的玉片流行于春秋战国时期，特
点是有纹饰的一面朝外，另一面向内为素面，四
角有穿孔，是缝缀在死者衣服上用于殓葬的，属
丧葬用玉。它是汉代玉衣的雏形。

This square or rectangular sheet-shaped jade pieces were
popular in the Spring-and-Autumn and Warring States Periods,
the features of which are that the obverse (outer side) bears
decorative patterns and the reverse (inner side) is plain and
perforations are found on the four corners. They were burial
jades sewn on the shrouds of the tomb occupants and can be
seen as the incipient form of the jade burial suits of the Han
Dynasty.

141 兽面纹玉片
Jade Plaque with Animal Mask Pattern

战国时期丧葬用玉
湖北省荆州市钟祥黄土坡墓地出土
高2.5、宽1.1~2.7、厚0.6厘米

Warring States Period
Excavated from Huangtupo Cemetery of
Chu State in Zhongxiang, Jingzhou, Hubei Province
H. 2.5 cm, W. 1.1~2.7 cm, Th. 0.6 cm

玉质黄色，不透明。上宽，下窄，呈不规则梯
形，两侧雕刻对称的扉棱。中间阴刻简化的兽面
纹及圆点纹。顶端有一圆穿孔。另一面素面。

142 玉俑
Jade Figurines (4 pieces)

战国时期丧葬用玉
湖北省荆州市紫荆砖瓦厂墓地出土
从左至右：灰黄色。高3.3、宽1厘米
青绿色，夹黑色及黄色斑。高4.3、宽1.4厘米
灰白色。高3.7、宽1.2厘米
黄绿色。高3.6、宽1厘米

Warring States Period
Excavated from Zijingzhuanwachang Cemetery of
Chu State in Jingzhou, Hubei Province
From left to right: H. 3.3 cm, W. 1 cm; H. 4.3 cm, W. 1.4 cm;
H. 3.7 cm, W. 1.2 cm; H. 3.6 cm, W. 1 cm;

4件。玉俑整体简略雕刻出人之头、肩及身体。菱
形头，一字形肩膀，身着长裙。

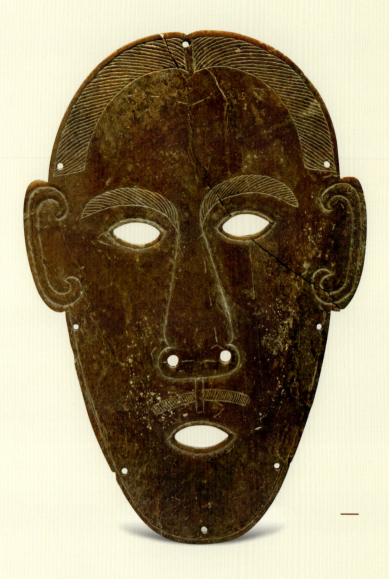

点　评
Commentary

玉面具也称"瞑目"、"面幕"，雕成人面及五官形状，是专门覆盖在死者面部的葬玉。它出现于西周，流行于春秋战国及西汉时期。一般常见的玉面具是将雕成人面五官的一些小玉件（如眼、眉、鼻、口、耳、胡须等）缝缀在织物上，覆盖于死者面部，而像这种整体雕刻出的人面玉面具极少见，它周边八个对称分布的小圆孔是为缝缀固定于织物上之用的。

The jade burial mask made into the shape of human face and facial organs (eyes, nose, mouth and ears) is the burial jade used for covering the face of the tomb occupant. It appeared in the Western Zhou Dynasty and became popular in the Spring-and-Autumn and Warring States Periods and the Western Han Dynasty. The eight symmetrically arranged small holes on its edge are for sewing to the textiles.

143　玉面具
Jade Funeral Mask

战国晚期丧葬用玉
湖北省荆州市秦家山墓地出土
长20、宽13.9、厚0.23厘米

Late Warring States Period
Excavated from Qinjiashan Cemetery of
Chu State in Jingzhou, Hubei Province
L. 20 cm, W. 13.9 cm, Th. 0.23 cm

玉质黄褐色。扁平体，椭圆形，两侧雕刻出两环形耳。头顶上部用阴刻的半圈斜线纹表现头发，同样用细密的斜线纹雕出柳叶形眉。两条阴刻的斜直线表现鼻翼，其上部和眉头相连。两耳阴刻卷云纹。用透雕方式雕刻出橄榄形眼，圆形鼻孔。鼻子和嘴巴之间用细密的斜线纹刻画胡子，造型生动。周边共八个小圆孔呈对称分布。

144 龙纹玉珠
Jade Bead with Dragon Pattern

战国时期玉佩饰
湖北省荆州市楚墓出土
高3.5、直径1.8、孔径0.3厘米

Warring States Period
Excavated from the Tombs of
Chu State in Jingzhou, Hubei Province
H. 3.5 cm ,D.(outer) 1.8 cm, D.(inner) 0.3 cm

玉质黄白色，微透明。橄榄形，两头小，中间
大，上下各有一周绹索纹，中间浅浮雕交缠龙
纹，纵向贯穿一个小圆孔。局部有残损。

145 琉璃珠
Glass Bead

战国时期琉璃佩饰
湖北省荆州市楚墓出土
高2.5、直径2.6、孔径0.7厘米

Warring States Period
Excavated from the Tombs of
Chu State in Jingzhou, Hubei Province
H. 2.5 cm , D.(outer) 2.6 cm, D.(inner) 0.7 cm

蓝色琉璃。椭圆球状，表面有凸起的乳钉状装饰。乳钉周边有三圈蓝色边线，乳钉中间有白色圆点装饰。

点 评
Commentary

春秋战国时期的琉璃珠俗称"蜻蜓眼"，可能是从西亚传来的"舶来品"。为何"蜻蜓眼"都是以蓝色为主呢？因为发明和使用琉璃的古埃及和两河流域的苏美尔人非常崇拜青金石饰品，如同中国人喜爱和田玉一样。当时青金石产地在今天的阿富汗，距古埃及有万里之遥，来之不易，故制作蓝色琉璃饰品以代替青金石，两者颜色非常近似，因此后来传入中国的"蜻蜓眼"就一律是深浅不一的蓝色琉璃制品。

The glass beads of the Spring-and-Autumn and Warring States Periods are usually called "eye beads", which were imported from the West Asia. The ancient Egyptians and Sumerians in Mesopotamia who invented glass-making technique admired the ornaments made of lapis lazuli; however, the lapis lazuli was produced in present-day Afghanistan faraway from Egypt and difficult to fetch, so the Egyptians made blue glass ornaments as substitutes, the color of which was very similar to that of lapis lazuli. Therefore, all of the "eye beads" imported into China were blue in various tints.

146 琉璃珠
Glass Bead

战国时期琉璃佩饰
湖北省荆州市楚墓出土
高1.4、直径1.8、孔径0.7厘米

Warring States Period
Excavated from the Tombs of
Chu State in Jingzhou, Hubei Province
H. 1.4 cm ,D.(outer) 1.8 cm, D.(inner) 0.7 cm

蓝色琉璃。圆鼓状，表面有白、黑地组成的小圆点装饰，顶部有一个小圆孔通到底部。

147 琉璃珠
Glass Bead

战国时期琉璃佩饰
湖北省荆州市楚墓出土
高3、直径2.4、孔径1厘米

Warring States Period
Excavated from the Tombs of
Chu State in Jingzhou, Hubei Province
H. 3 cm, D.(outer) 2.4 cm, D.(inner) 1 cm

深蓝色琉璃。算珠形，用白底和蓝地勾勒出六瓣
花朵，外围用黄色线条勾勒。装饰之间用白色条
状带连接。连接处有黄色圆点装饰。

148 琉璃珠
Glass Bead

战国时期琉璃佩饰
湖北省荆州市楚墓出土
高3.5、直径1.6、孔径0.6厘米

Warring States Period
Excavated from the Tombs of
Chu State in Jingzhou, Hubei Province
H. 3.5 cm , D.(outer) 1.6 cm, D.(inner) 0.6 cm

深蓝色琉璃。长椭圆柱状，中部略内凹。表面有
三周弦纹及白底蓝色圆点纹。

149 琉璃珠
Glass Bead

战国时期琉璃佩饰
湖北省荆州市楚墓出土
高2.1、直径2.2、孔径0.7厘米

Warring States Period
Excavated from the Tombs of
Chu State in Jingzhou, Hubei Province
H. 2.1 cm, D.(outer) 2.2 cm, D.(inner) 0.7 cm

蓝色琉璃。圆球状，饰大、小圆点纹，其上有蓝
色镶嵌。部分已脱落。

150 紫晶珠
Amethyst Bead

战国早期水晶佩饰
湖北省荆州市熊家冢墓地出土
长3、孔径0.6厘米

Early Warring States Period
Excavated from Xiongjiazhong Cemetery of
Chu State in Jingzhou, Hubei Province
L. 3 cm, D.(inner) 0.6 cm

紫色水晶，透明。椭圆球状，两头小，中间大，
两端各有一个圆孔，为双面钻孔，中间有错位痕
及裂痕。

151 紫晶管串饰
A String of Amethyst Tubular Beads

战国早期水晶佩饰
湖北省荆州市熊家冢墓地出土
由21枚紫色水晶管组成，每枚直径约0.8、长约1.7厘米

Early Warring States Period
Excavated from Xiongjiazhong Cemetery of
Chu State in Jingzhou, Hubei Province
L. 1.7 cm, D. 0.8 cm (each piece)

紫色水晶，透明。圆柱体，两侧都有穿孔，为双
面钻孔。大部分玉管两侧都有局部的断裂。

152 石料
A Piece of Quartz with Cutting Traces

战国时期
湖北省荆州市郢城镇出土

Warring States Period
Excavated from Yingchengzhen Site of
Chu State in Jingzhou, Hubei Province

石英岩质，灰白色，表面呈波浪状凸凹不平，边
缘有人工切割痕，内质有孔隙。

玉器主要纹饰
Patterns of Jades

———

玉质颜色
Colors of Jades

———

玉器沁色
Erosion Colors of Jades

附 录
APPENDIXES

附录1　玉器主要纹饰
Appendix I　Patterns of Jades

| 谷纹　Grain Pattern | 勾连谷纹　Grain Pattern |

| 圆涡纹　Whirlpool Pattern | 勾连云纹　Cloud Pattern |

乳钉纹　Nipple Pattern

蝌蚪纹　Tadpole Pattern

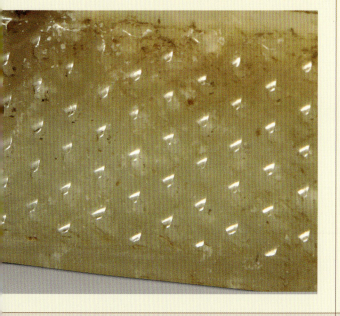

卷云纹　Cloud Pattern

几何形云纹　Cloud Pattern

"S"形云纹　S-shaped Cloud Pattern	蟠虺纹　Coiled Dragon Pattern

网格纹　Grid Pattern	绚索纹　Rope Pattern

兽面纹　Animal Mask Pattern

龙首纹　Dragon Head Pattern

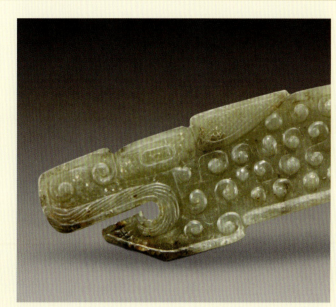

绞丝纹　Rope Pattern

连续三角纹
Triangle Pattern

斜线纹
Slash Grain Pattern

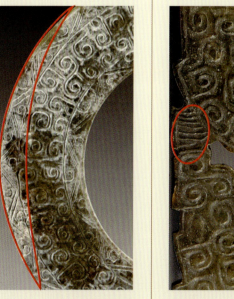

附录2 玉质颜色
Appendix II Colors of Jades

白色（乳白色） White

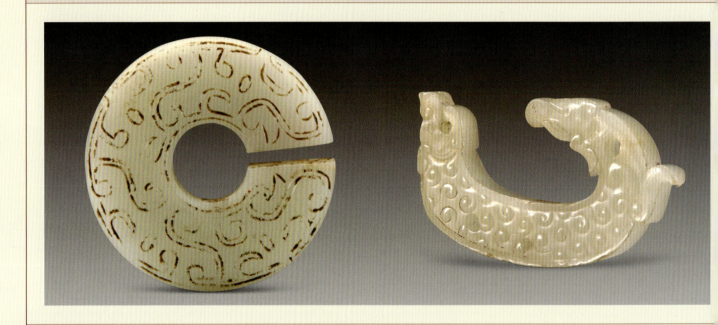

青白色 Green white

黄白色　Yellow-white

黄绿色　Yellow-green

青绿色　Cyan

红褐色　Reddish-brown

绿色（碧绿、深绿） Green

黄褐色 Tan	黑色 Black

附录3　玉器沁色
Appendix III　Erosion Colors of Jades

灰白色　Gray

灰黄色　Sallow

鸡骨白　Chicken　Bone

黄褐色　Tan

红褐色　Reddish-brown

灰黑色　Gray and black

黑褐色　Dark　brown

黑色　Black

后　记
POSTSCRIPT

　　自2006年以来，荆州熊家冢楚王陵考古发掘工作取得重大成果，殉葬墓中出土了近2000件玉器，这为认识战国时期楚国玉器的面貌提供了宝贵资料，也是编纂和出版本书的契机。2009年，在荆州博物馆馆长王明钦和玉器专家古方策划和组织下，调集考古工作者、库房和陈列管理人员以及摄影专家组成联合研究组，对该馆所藏出土楚国玉器进行了全面的整理和研究。这部图录就是历时三年研究成果的结晶。

　　本图录在编写和出版过程中还得到了很多玉器爱好者及中国收藏家协会学术研究部的倾力支持，他们多次观摩荆州博物馆馆藏玉器，资助本图录出版，为弘扬和传承中国源远流长的玉文化尽了绵薄之力，谨此向孙璇、石清、杨文丽、杨希、王玮、王燕、陈利娟致谢。

编　者

2012年9月

责任编辑：张征雁
责任印制：张道奇
装帧设计：雁　翎

图书在版编目（CIP）数据

荆州楚玉：湖北荆州出土战国时期楚国玉器 ／ 荆州
博物馆编著.—北京：文物出版社，2012.10（2015.7重印）
　　ISBN 978-7-5010-3529-8

　　Ⅰ.①荆…　Ⅱ.①荆…　Ⅲ.①古玉器－研究－荆州市
－楚国（？～前223）　Ⅳ.①K876.84

　　中国版本图书馆CIP数据核字(2012)第203561号

荆州楚玉—— 湖北荆州出土战国时期楚国玉器

编　　著　荆州博物馆
出版发行　文物出版社
　　　　　（北京市东直门内北小街 2 号楼　邮政编码 100007）
　　　　　http://www.wenwu.com
　　　　　E-mail：web@wenwu.com
制版印刷　北京图文天地制版印刷有限公司
经　　销　新华书店
开　　本　889×1194　1/16
印　　张　13
版　　次　2012年10月第1版　2015年7月第2次印刷
书　　号　ISBN 978-7-5010-3529-8

定　　价　320.00元